Dean Carey is an intelligent and creative teacher and theatre person; his rapport with his students is marvellous.

Robert Benedetti, California Institute of the Arts

Full of such essential truth that it seems at once revelatory and confirmatory. This book will give the actor a massive injection of self-confidence at the same time propelling them into unknown territory. An affirmation of the actor's great strength – instinct. Buy it!

Hugo Weaving, Actor

Surely the final journey for the actor is the personal, the exploration of the instinct – 'to be as good as *I* can be'. At last a book to help me on my way.

Marcus Graham, Actor

This book is filled with catalysts to fire your imagination, expand your awareness and galvanise your will. Buy this book and you will never work alone again!

Lindy Davies, Theatre Director

This book is a 'must read' for any actor facing auditions, not only because it is practical, helpful and full of good ideas, but because Dean's entertaining examples and inspiring insight unite us all in a common love for the work and an aspiration to do our very best.

Gale Edwards, Theatre Director

For auditionees and performers interested in an intelligent and insightful analysis of the state of theatrical practice, this book is essential and profitable reading.

Wayne Harrison, Director, Sydney Theatre Company

Masterclass revitalises all those basic acting impulses you keep forgetting, with a precision, ease and common sense that is stimulating and reassuring. A masterful work.

John Bell, The Bell Shakespeare Company

Dean's book stokes the seers within, it reminds us why we are actors. It is universally valuable to me – whether I am auditioning in Sydney, New York or LA.

Gia Carides, Actor

DEAN CAREY has been involved extensively in theatrical education for over 14 years. He has taught for the AFTRS, the Nimrod Company, Belvoir Street Theatre and the NSW Conservatorium. He taught at NIDA for five years and was Associate Head of Acting. He was then appointed Head of Acting at the WA Academy of Performing Arts where, over his four-year stay, he directed *A Month in the Country*, *Peer Gynt, Dark of the Moon, Flora the Red Menace, The Rover* and *The Golden Age*. He also directed *Savage Love, The Touch of Silk, Late Arrivals, Sunrise, Children of the Sun* and *Tales From the Vienna Woods*.

He has conducted guest workshops throughout the US at the University of California in San Diego, CalArts and the University of Southern California in Los Angeles, The American Conservatory Theatre in San Francisco, Ensemble Theatre Company in Florida and the Los Angeles High School of Performing Arts. Dean also works as a dialogue coach and performance consultant in the film and television industries.

In 1986 he established The Actor's Centre in Sydney, a professional development base for industry workers and students of acting. Its charter was, and still is, to facilitate the extension of essential skills and to enhance the performer's productivity.

In that same year his first book, *The Actor's Audition Manual*, was published by Currency Press and has since sold over 12,000 copies.

MASTERCLASS

THE ACTOR'S AUDITION MANUAL

WOMEN

Dean Carey

HEINEMANN
PORTSMOUTH, NEW HAMPSHIRE

First published in 1995 by
Currency Press, P.O. Box 452,
Paddington, NSW 2021, Australia.

Published simultaneously in the USA by Heinemann
A Division of Reed Publishing (USA) Inc.,
361 Hanover Street,
Portsmouth, NH 03801-3912
Offices and Agents throughout the world.

Distributed in Canada By Reed Books Canada,
204 Richmond Street West, Suite 300,
Toronto, Ontario M5V 1V6
This edition is not for sale in Australia, New Zealand, or Europe.

CIP catalogue records for this book are available from the British Library and the Library of Congress

ISBN 0-435-08679-0 (Women)
ISBN 0-435-08678-2 (Men)

Typeset by Currency and The Master Typographer
Printed in Australia by Southwood Press, Sydney, NSW
Cover design by Anaconda Graphic Design

Preface

This book is a companion to *The Actor's Audition Manual,* first published in 1985. In Part One of this book you will find important updates on the art of auditioning, as well as fresh information to help re-direct your energies and allow maximum benefit from every audition opportunity.

In Part Two, using speeches as examples, we'll explore in detail a range of exercises which may challenge the way you work on your piece. A number of powerful and *practical* ways are fully illustrated, which aim to release the speech's dynamic range and increase your sense of personal ownership. They will prove an invaluable stimulus and resource when rehearsing and preparing. They will energise your approach and encourage your creative drive.

In Part Three you will find a collection of around one hundred monologues for theatre auditions *and* film and television screen tests. Many actors are now being asked to present rehearsed pieces for screen tests, and some of the speeches in Part Three have been selected especially for this environment. Collected over the last seven years, these monologues present a wide range of exciting possibilities for you to practise your art.

I thank the countless number of actors who, through their commitment and courage in my workshops, have helped design and develop the exercises in this book to their present form. I am sure your work will benefit as a result and you will fulfil your desire to discover more about the craft, that leads toward the art.

Dean Carey, Sydney 1995

Striking the balance between the technique and the adventure...

Contents

Copyright Acknowledgments

Fair Slaughter by Howard Barker from *Crimes in Hot Countries/Fair Slaughter*, published by John Calder (Publisher) Ltd. and reproduced by permission of the playwright and The Calder Educational Trust, London. • *A Chip in the Sugar* by Alan Bennett, Reprinted by permission of the Peters Fraser and Dunlop Group Ltd. • *Decadence, East* and *Greek* by Steven Berkoff, *Decadence* © Steven Berkoff 1981, 1982, 1983, 1986, 1989, *East* © Steven Berkoff 1977, 1978, 1982, 1989, *Greek* © Steven Berkoff 1980, 1982, 1983, 1986, 1989, by permission of Rosica Colin Ltd. • *Laughing Wild* by Christopher Durang, © Christopher Durang 1988 by permission of Grove/Atlantic, Inc. • *Statements after an Arrest Under the Immortality Act* by Athol Fugard, Copyright by Athol Fugard, by permission of Sheil Land Associates Ltd. • *Camille* in *Three Plays* by Pam Gems, copyright © Pam Gems, 1985. Reproduced by permission of Penguin Books Ltd. • *Yes and After* from *Three Plays* by Michael Hastings, copyright © Michael Hastings, 1962, reproduced by permission of Penguin Books Ltd. • *Boy's Life and Other Plays* by Howard Korder, © 1989 Howard Korder by permission of Grove/Atlantic, Inc. • *Angels in America - Part One: Millennium Approaches* by Tony Kushner, Copyright © 1992 Tony Kushner, reproduced by permission of Nick hern Books, London. • *Angels in America - Part Two: Perestroika* by Tony Kushner, Copyright © 1994 Tony Kushner, reproduced by permission of Nick Hern Books, London. • *Play with a Tiger* by Doris Lessing, Copyright © 1962 Doris Lessing Productions Ltd. Reprinted by permission of Jonathon Clowes Ltd., London, on behalf of Doris Lessing. • *All My Sons* by Arthur Miller, Copyright, 1947, by Arthur Miller, Copyright Renewed, 1974 by Arthur Miller, by permission of DRAMATIST PLAY SERVICES, INC. • *The Bells of Hell* by John Mortimer, Reprinted by permission of the Peters Fraser and Dunlop Group Ltd. • *Hurlyburly* by David Rabe, Copyright 1985 by Ralko Corp, by permission of Grove/Atlantic, Inc. • *The One Day of the Year* by Alan Seymour, Reprinted by permission of Angus and Robertson Bay Books. • *Five Finger Exercise* from *Three Plays* by Peter Shaffer, copyright © Peter Shaffer, 1958, reproduced by permission of Penguin Books Ltd. • *Lovers and Other Strangers* by Renee Taylor and Joseph Bolonga, Copyright 1968 by Renee Taylor and Joseph Bolonga by permission of Samuel French, Inc. • *Les Belles-soeurs* by Michel Tremblay; translation copyright © 1992 John Van Burek and Bill Glassco; Talon Books Ltd, Vancouver, B.C., Canada. • *On the Eve* by Ivan Sergeyevich Turgenev, translated by Gilbert Gardiner copyright © Gilbert Gardiner, 1950, reproduced by permission of Penguin Books Ltd. • *Loose Ends* by Michael Weller, Copyright 1979, 1980 by Michael Weller by permission of Samuel French, Inc. • *Lady Othello* from *Lady Othello and Other Plays* and *The Friends* from *Chips with Everything and Other Plays* by Arnold Wesker, *Lady Othello* copyright © Arnold Wesker, 1990, *The Friends* copyright © Arnold Wesker 1970, reproduced by permission of Penguin Books Ltd.

Acknowledgments

I would like to sincerely thank Dr. Geoffrey Gibbs and all his staff at the Western Australia Academy of Performing Arts – particularly Lisle Jones. His intimate knowledge of the craft of acting and the passion it takes to be an artist has helped to establish WAAPA as one of the leading national acting institutions. I have felt privileged to be associated with a disciplined and nurturing educational facility which produces students whose attitude and approach to the industry is respected by all professionals.

Many thanks are due to my research assistant, Mary-Anne Gifford, whose tireless efforts culminated in the collating of over five hundred speeches in over 110 degree heat.

Thanks yet again to the staff at the NIDA library for their assistance and welcome support.

Both the Performing Arts and Ariel Bookshops in Sydney also offered their guidance and help.

Finally, thankyou to the following people for their encouragement and advice; Bob Griffiths, Tony Knight, Chris Edmund, Glenn B. Swift, Monique Spanbrook, and Lisa Schouw.

Photographic Credits

PLATE 1 Photo: Jon Green; Actor: Lisa Baumwol • PLATE 2 Photo: Jon Green; Actor: Roxane Wilson • PLATE 3 Photo: Terry Smith; Actor: Heidi Lapaine • PLATE 4 Photo: Eric Sierins; Actors: John Adam & Deborah Galanos • PLATE 5 Photo: Jon Green; Actors: Hugh Jackson & Dean Carey • PLATE 6 Photo: Jon Green; Actors: Jennifer Botica & Dean Carey • PLATE 7 Photo: Jon Green; Actors: Jennifer Botica & Dean Carey • PLATE 8 Photo: Terry Smith; Actors: Journey Students • PLATE 9 Photo: Jon Green; Actors: (*l.* to *r.*) Simon Lyndon, Lisa Baumwol, Wadih Dona, Lucille Reynolds, Ben Harkin, Marin Mimica, Natasha McNamara, Dominic Purcell • PLATE 10 Photo: Branco Gaica; Actors: Lisa Bailey and Damian Pike.

PART ONE

The Path to Process

Chapter 1

Road Testing

The Bottom Line

You have an audition coming up. Yes, you will have to *act.* There's no doubt about it. You might chat for a while, discuss future projects, speak of your 'life in art' but, at some stage without fail, they're going to say, 'Act!'.

Unfortunately, unlike other creative artists, you have chosen an art form which will not be satisfied with a piece of pottery, a painting on canvas, a sequenced sound or a stone sculpture to allow its release. It uses *you. You* are its vehicle. You can't create wildly in the privacy of your own home — trying, testing, experimenting — then after completion, send off the demo tape or invite the prospective buyers and dealers to your gallery showing. You front up and *become* your own product.

All things being equal, the audition may go well and be very acceptable. Your personal 'product launch' may have been charming, skilful and efficient, proving yet again your ability to understand what was required and as a result, deliver the goods. But did your selection resonate with your stamp of truth? Did it speak in ways which *revealed* you? Was it a personal statement affecting *change* within you and those watching?

The Authentic Self

We all want our work to resound with our uniqueness. What then prohibits or inhibits this from happening? Jacques Copeau, one of France's most prolific actors, directors and theatricians, strode into his office at the Theatre du Vieux Colombier after directing a rehearsal, frustrated and at a crossroad:

> Did you see them again today? I always know in advance what they are going to do. They cannot get out of themselves. They reduce

everything to the level of their own habits, their cliches, their affectations. They do not invent anything. It is all sheer imitation of imitation. [1]

Why do we succumb to this imitation? So often it seems our focus falls on *trying to get it right* — we attempt to present a suitable form which will 'read' as appropriate to those viewing. We deliver a set of polished and efficient acting 'signals' to successfully demonstrate our ability and talent. This accent on form can be extremely lethal to our sense of invention and our instinctive personal investment.

Our strong need to get it right, to do what will be acceptable, to have the correct vocal and physical qualities in order that the work be seen as 'valid', compounds this imitation. Once there, our uniqueness deserts us and is replaced by a highly polished exterior or shell, encasing what we have created and leaving our performance bereft of its pure interior truth.

After an exercise I often ask the actors to state, on a scale of one to ten, how *correct* they were aiming to be. Many say between seven and ten. I then ask, on the same scale, 'How active was your *instinct*?' The answer is often 'three'. The reason? The actors were focusing once again on trying to achieve what they believed were *my* wishes or the results *I* was looking for. As a result, imitation emerges and the authentic self is silenced.

I then ask the actors what could they do to allow their level three instinct to be *doubled*? After a few searching moments where they reorder their priorities, they answer: 'Forget about you... follow my impulses... physicalise more'. We then repeat the scene. This time the actors' attention rests firmly on the precise and accurate directions they have given themselves. Consequently, their work departs from the world of imitation, from 'this is what it *would* be like *if* I was feeling...' to 'this is what it *is* like to feel...'.

The work speaks with much more individuality as the actors develop a reality based on their *instincts* and *honesty*. The learning that results becomes far more valuable to the actors because it has been *their* discovery and clarification of *their* individual processes. For acting cannot be taught, only learnt.

My task as a teacher is to provide the most potent opportunities in which actors can become more intimate with their creative process — what undermines and thwarts it, what affirms and accelerates it. I believe *this* to be the most effective contribution I can make to each developing artist.

In summary, there are two distinct modes actors work within — one is the *inventing* mode, where they aim to please and impress, the other is the *responding* mode, where they allow themselves to react and experience. If an actor is working to invent, I often ask them to do the first eight lines of the scene where their sole focus is to please *me*. Then we repeat the first eight lines with the sole focus being to please *themselves*. I then ask which feels more effective? The key is to work towards self-satisfaction through creative autonomy.

The Court is Now in Session

One reason actors lose their self-trust and become separated from their inner 'hunch' is that many believe the teacher knows how it should be played and that they don't. It's very necessary for every actor to realise that the teacher, and indeed director, often *doesn't know* how the scene should look, sound and feel. All they are sure about is that the potent cocktail of circumstances surrounding the characters should promote a series of dynamic exchanges. As the actors react to these circumstances, so does the director. Then together the cast and director edit and craft these various choices of reaction, to eventually produce meaning — the production's *vision*.

With the belief that the person out front 'knows it all', the actor's job becomes more of a trial — a series of long days second-guessing and end-gaining in order to validate their casting and eventually, their self-worth. Once you release yourselves from this crippling approach, rehearsals become an expedition where creative discovery and fulfilment once again become possible.

The entire thrust of my teaching over the past twelve years has been towards unearthing ways of releasing the actor from the *limits* of imitation. By offering you the opportunity to connect with the purity of the work, it is hoped that you may ultimately replace product with *process*, results with *evolution* and predetermining with *perception*.

The exercises in this book are therefore designed to:

- activate an organic, physical life
- promote deep personal connections
- extend the boundaries of your unique expression.

This book will offer active and potent ways to enable you to shed the sense of 'correctness' which many actors aim for, so that your instinctive and intuitive self may achieve full disclosure through your work. We will also look closely at structure, function, playwright's intention, and what Stanislavsky called the actor's *score*. Without this score, you're relying on luck and 'feeling right' on the night. Danger! We all know that the purity and permission we *privately* allow ourselves can be robbed from us by anything which makes us feel self-conscious. In an audition there are countless dynamics around us which, if plugged into, will lead us quite successfully to feeling nothing *but* self-conscious. As you will see in the chapters ahead, the actor's score carefully crafts each moment in order to establish a confident and solid knowledge of the inner workings of the character and the surrounding scene. As Stanislavsky said:

> the artist... must be the master of his own inspiration and must know how to call it forth at the hour announced on the posters of the theatre. This is the chief secret of our art.[2]

To Repeat or Not to Repeat

The actor's job is twofold — to be capable of *repeating* every moment and to be able to *justify* all action.

Without the score of your scene — the precise plotting of the character's moment-by-moment journey — you run the enormous risk of being a legend in your lounge room, but feeling a non-entity in the audition room.

> Inspiration comes and goes – adrenalin can get you through, but quickly fades with constant use...

Technique and skill can ensure *accurate repetition* and therefore *re-creation.*

> Technique without instinct is hollow. Instinct without technique is blind.[3]

Your score defines your work and gives your instinct the foundation from which to fly.

In Part Two, The Creative Arena, we will look at audition speeches and uncover their scores. This will provide a solid base from which you can activate your instinctive powers.

The Job of Justifying

The audience needs to see *reasons* for the character's actions. The actor must then *own* these reasons sufficiently so as to allow the actions, thoughts and emotions to spring from this inner source.

Let's take an imaginary scene: Man One runs onto the stage, shouts, leaps for joy, and yells 'Life is fine!' Woman One enters wielding a chainsaw, cuts out his heart and screams 'Revenge!'. Blackout.

Not a play I'd particularly stand in line to see, but in order to act Man One, you must justify it all — the run, the leap, the choice of words and all the circumstances prior to his entry. These may include six years of marriage leading to divorce, the guilt, turmoil and anguish of leaving his wife, his eventual escape to a tropical hide-out and now, the imminent and long-awaited arrival of his new lover. He may finally feel, for the first time in his life, that all is at last well, and life is indeed 'fine'.

Ownership

You not only have to justify but you must *personalise* each circumstance. You must create personal *connections* to every word, idea, action, emotion and gesture your character inhabits if you're to create a vivid and defined stage life.

An actor friend went for a role in an episode of the TV series *A Country Practice*. The character description was 'distraught mother': she had lost her child through cot death. As a result of her distress she had fainted and split open her head. We see her in the casualty area of the local hospital — obviously 'distraught' and in great pain and shock. She is attended to with care and understanding by the doctor and a number of nurses who admit her for observation overnight. The next morning the doctor arrives by her bedside and asks 'And how are you today?' She replies, 'Better — I feel slightly better this morning... (taking the doctor's hand) thankyou'.

To say that one line in your performance you may have to imaginatively connect to, and therefore personalise, the following: the first time you met your husband, the first date, the decision to marry, moving into the house, discovery of the pregnancy, painting the nursery, hanging the mobiles above the cot, the trauma and elation of giving birth, the first touch of the child's skin, the first look into its eyes, leaving hospital with the child, tucking it into its new bed, the newness and special quality of that first week, and then finally, the devastating and horrific pre-dawn discovery of the baby's death.

You'll be asked to act many situations which you have never had any experience of. This is where you enter the world of the imagined — Stanislavsky's 'magic if'. *If* I lived in the same circumstance as the character, *if* I had the same background, age, social status, outlook, and *if* these events happened to me, how would *I* feel, think, react?

> 'If' acts as a lever to lift us out of the world of actuality and into the realm of the imagination.[4]

It is within this world that secret and hidden truths lie. We as actors have access to this world and because of this, our art can flourish.

This imaginative exploration becomes the springboard to our onstage reality. Our words, actions, ideas and emotions begin as imagined, for they are not our own. But the journey is one of claiming them, decoding them, embracing them and then lastly being transformed by them. This is often called 'grounding' the work.

To help form this essential foundation it is wise to start from the nucleus of truth within you: *you* are a human being, so too is your character. Therefore, there must be parts of the character and yourself which cross over. To pinpoint this mutual emotional fibre, ask what universal *wants* you share with your character: control, survival, power, freedom, love, respect. Allow these elemental human needs to connect the emotions of the play to your own. In short, you hook up to the forces driving the character and in turn create an emotional fusion between their world and your own.

The *process* of personalisation differs greatly from actor to actor. Some prefer to imagine in minute detail every aspect of the character's situation. With appropriate music as an underscore, they might lie on the floor and run an imaginary film through their head — emotionally exploring and subsequently investing each and every frame with meaning and consequence.

Others write letters or poetry as if from the character's hand. This process of articulating on paper the precise interior state and perspective of the character allows the actor to understand the human cost and emotional significance of each moment.

Talking to people who have experienced or witnessed the exact or similar circumstances can be a key and major stimulus for the actor. Artworks, films, novels, journals, sculpture, music — all of these can transport you from the world of actuality and into the realm of your imagination. They can fuse the actor's and character's connection to the situation. This then particularises, humanises and *personalises* each dynamic thread which, when woven together, reveal the character in relation to their world.

Remember: Approaches such as these and the many exercises in the chapters to follow are designed to be used *if* instinct isn't enough. Techniques are there to support, not replace, instinct. You must keep reminding yourselves of this. Trust in your inner hunch — be courageous and follow your initial impulses and instincts. If necessary, use techniques as triggers, as strategies. 'The first aspect of the method (any method) is to get the unconscious to work. The second is, once it starts, to leave it alone.' [5]

Naturally

For whatever reason, you may be able to play the role with ease — justifying all behaviour and connecting to the feelings behind the dialogue *instantly.* Sometimes we 'know' the material, we intuitively feel we could play this role. So, 'if it 'ain't broke, don't fix it'.

But if it isn't exactly broken but it's also not state of the art, then some personal exploration of the interior landscape of the character becomes vital. For a one-line moment in a television episode I wouldn't suggest weeks of research and living-in at your local hospital. But some specific work to stimulate the imagination and help claim the material may prove to be invaluable. Through your ability to fill in and flesh out every detail you start to become physically and emotionally *transformed.* To allow this transformation to take place you must essentially have ownership of the character's circumstances and their world. Ultimately, this requires a *personal investment* on your behalf.

Exposure

Some actors fear the 'exposure' of some part of themselves. They fear that the pain or joy or hatred of their character may be misinterpreted as *them* releasing some part of *their* inner feelings. This concern stifles and inhibits many actors and robs them of the wealth of human experience within them. It leads them to abandon their authentic self and to act through the imitation discussed earlier.

In a class, rehearsal or audition you may reveal quite strong and deep personal feelings or connections to the material. Quite powerful resonances may be felt as a result of the collision (or indeed collusion) between the material and yourself. But this personal exposure need never concern you. Why? Because, as Lisle Jones once said in a class at the Academy, the audience will *never know* — they will only ever think it's good acting.

Student actors can also feel threatened by the demands of the work. The intense expectation to 'reveal' or to 'risk' can be daunting. I once heard it said that actors are actors because their souls are close to the surface. There is truth in this. There are times when the character's pain is your pain, his or her fears, yours. Relax in the knowledge that you have a full-time safety net — people are looking for, and hoping to see, good acting.

When your work resonates due to your personal attachments and the atmosphere which surrounds you becomes charged through your personal exposure, your acting becomes *informed.* Those watching will applaud your *craft*, regardless of where it may have been forged.

In the following chapter we will look at the nature of the creative process and discuss ways to engage these personal links in all we do.

Chapter 2

The Creative State

The Secret Fear

'All right', I hear you say, 'what if I create from my *authentic self*, I expose my truth informed by the very depth of my imagination, and... it doesn't work? People don't applaud the event. The risk *doesn't* pay off. I *don't* get the job!!!' You may think perhaps, it's better to simply imitate the appropriate and remain safe, rather than sorry. This approach can be seductive and, when fuelled by fear, can greatly undermine your true creative potential.

We certainly haven't chosen an easy task and in our art form there are no sure solutions. We are throwing our hat into the ring every time we perform.

So often in interviews with internationally acclaimed artists you hear them express the same fear — that *this* time they'll be found out for sure! Somehow the next project will expose them as an impostor and a fraud. They'll be publicly humiliated then ostracised for all eternity. Even though things may have been going *quite* well for *quite* some time with, dare I say, *quite* an amount of success, *this* time, all will be revealed in a blaze of embarrassing mediocrity.

And why shouldn't you feel this? Every job or task you undertake is unique — a one-off. Just when you get the hang of a role, the season closes and you find yourself thrust into another alien situation where nothing is tangible and all is at stake and at risk... again. A new play, new actors, a new director, a different vision to follow, a new life form for you to make real so that within five or so weeks of rehearsal, it will walk and talk and people won't run screaming from the theatre! The only common thread that is woven through this succession of challenges is that very familiar fear — *this* time, it could all go wrong.

What can be said? It's part of the terrain. It comes with the territory. Every artist feels it, to a greater or lesser extent, constantly. If you *didn't*, then what would your art consist of? It would be safe, perhaps smug, self-content. It would be without risk, self-investment, personal truth. Would you wish to be in a profession which *didn't* embrace these qualities?

The Courage to Create

In his book entitled *Creativity*, C.R. Rogers talks about the internal opposites at work during the creative process. The first is what he calls the 'Eureka feeling: 'This is *it*!'; 'I have discovered!'; 'This is what I wanted to express!'.

The second he calls 'the anxiety of separateness'. He explains that he does not believe that many significant creative products are formed without the feelings: 'I am alone. No one has ever done just this before. I have ventured into territory where no one has been. Perhaps I am foolish, or wrong, or lost, or abnormal'.

So you're in good company! During the creative process we *all* feel this inner friction. But we continue nevertheless. Through this internal turmoil, where foolishness and chaos abide, our need to externalise ourselves through a creative statement prevails. Some say that art is the search for clarity and resolution. For many of us this search is ongoing.

The next challenge to our inner belief is a *post*-creative one: how, *after* we create, do we *evaluate* our work? What do we focus upon when everyone around us has their definitive opinion and exacting personal taste?

> Perhaps the most fundamental condition of creativity is that the source of evaluative judgment is internal. The value of the product is, for the creative person, established not by the praise or criticism of others, but by ourselves. Have I created something satisfying to *me*? Does it express part of me — my feeling or my thought, my pain or my ecstasy? These are the only questions which really matter to the creative person.
>
> This does not mean that we are oblivious to, or unwilling to be aware of, the judgment of others. It is simply that the basis of evaluation lies within ourself, in our own organismic reaction to and appraisal of our product. If to the person it has the 'feel' of being 'me in action', of being an actualisation of potentialities in ourself which heretofore have not existed and are now emerging into existence, then it is satisfying and creative, and no outside evaluation can change that fundamental fact.[6]

Only with this attitude can you forge ahead, continuing your quest for creative expression through affirming the partnership between who you are and what you create.

Archaeological

Leaving aside external criticism or praise (for some of us, this is the easiest input to place in perspective), what happens if *you* believe your work and effort wasn't a true reflection of your potential? For whatever reason, *you* were unsatisfied?

Firstly, you must acknowledge that once you've created something — presented your audition, which is an act of creation — that creation is finished. It has been completed. For what you created was only a reflection of where you were at, at that exact moment in your life. It was a point in the process. If your creative process is to *continue* you must now move on, allowing your ever-growing knowledge and perception to inform your work. Otherwise you can become anchored to that moment — a creative history repeating itself and producing a cycle lacking in freshness and naivety.

I once saw a production called *Archaeological* at the Sydney Performance Space, in which one of the performers had designed, constructed and then played his own instruments. He stood in a tight, overhead smoky spotlight and raised a small and beautifully crafted clay pipe to his lips. From the silence came a delicate and haunting sound. The very air surrounding him seemed to vibrate.

After the last long note gently faded, he took the pipe from his lips, raised it up as if in reverence, then allowed it to slip from his fingers and shatter on the floor below. His creative gesture had served its purpose. He now moved on to craft another vehicle in which to channel his creative impulse.

The same is true of your work. Some actors hold onto past 'failures' (and sometimes successes) and become doomed to repeat the pattern by not approaching each new task with freshness and genuine spontaneity. The act of creation must be a response to where you are at as a person at that time. The sum of your personal energies and life-force at that instant in your life produces a play, a poem, a piece of pottery, a role in a production. As you move through your work, you grow, develop and change. This is unavoidable. Your creative gestures *will* be renewed by this journey *if* you embrace each step and give yourselves the courage and the *permission* to keep creating.

In other words, the adventure continues...

Original Sin

> Creativity is the surrender of the infinite possibilities on the altar of form.[7]

In a sense, this may be true. But each time we work we face the thrill and challenge of playing with, and losing ourselves in, the infinite possibilities *without* being bound by a preconceived idea of the form our creativity should ultimately take. Obviously there will come a time when the choices we have made must be justified in terms of serving the story and fulfilling what we believe to be the playwright's intentions.

Initially however, what do you need to focus on... being creative?, clever?, original?, unique? Unfortunately, striving for these qualities can easily condemn an actor to a miserable life of repetition. In our often manic and vain attempt to be 'original' we focus on what has worked in the past or what we 'once saw', which may now be applicable if repeated. We then regurgitate old patterns within patterns, creating imitation upon imitation.

Remember — you are the only person in the world who looks like you and has had the same background, upbringing, education, cultural conditioning and experiences. How much more original do you want to be? Therefore, attempting to be 'creative' can easily lead to a focus on form rather than on content, and can stifle the ease with which you wish to work. Only by surrendering your need to know what may happen, how your piece should look and sound, and by following your organic impulses, will a free exploration and a pure creative release occur. Remember: process not product; content over form.

Basically, you have two choices: to *act* based on what you've seen or done before, or to *react* based on what you think and feel *now*. The hardest thing can be to get some actors to stop worrying and controlling what they think *should* happen, and to surrender and experience what *is* happening.

Part Two of this book offers a host of opportunities to launch your imagination, based on what you *think* and *feel* — in essence, reconnecting to your authentic self.

Permission to Play

A useful strategy to avoid the burden of trying to be original is to find ways of enabling yourself to toy with elements and concepts instead of having a fixed attitude about what you wish to achieve:

> Associated with the openness and lack of rigidity... is the ability to play spontaneously with ideas, colours, shapes, relationships — to juggle elements into impossible juxtapositions, to shape wild hypotheses, to make the given problematic, to express the ridiculous, to translate from one form to another... it is from this spontaneous toying and exploration that there arises the hunch, the creative seeing of life in a new and significant way. It is as though out of the wasteful spawning of thousands of possibilities there emerges one or two evolutionary forms with the qualities which give them a more permanent value.[8]

So to create freely you must give yourselves the *permission to play*. You must release your grip on form and shape and enter the arena of 'what could be'. From this vantage point, your invention can become limitless.

The Essential Source

In 1991 I had the privilege of teaching at the truly extraordinary Shchukin Higher Theatre School of the Vakhtangov State Academic Theatre in Moscow. It was to be a remarkable experience.

The ride from the airport was just as I had imagined: scenes of bleakness, desolation and aimlessness, as if all the colour had drained from the sky, land and people; incredible sights of huge, stolid towers of flats — all grey, uniform, certain and strong, yet dilapidated and on the verge of decay. Sounds of gunshots became fireworks as the city celebrated Anti-Aircraft Day. I stood by the Moscow River in the bitter cold to witness this synchronised display launched from over twenty locations — organised, precise, constrained. As the night sky exploded all around it was as if a brutal war had begun without warning. Then, just as abruptly, the sky dissolved into flames of orange and smoke.

This was certainly a welcome beyond any other. What was I to expect from the actors?! A fierce grip on form and product? A technical rigidity? Too much command and control over their energy as a result of their strict discipline? What would they make of *my* work?

The building the class took place in was more like an old ballroom — crumbling, raw, full of history. We climbed the fourteen sets of stairs and entered the rehearsal room on the top floor. With my translator at the ready, I mustered my forces and began the class.

I was right: they *were* technical masters of their bodies which are their instruments, accurate and precise. But their skills were matched with another passionate belief: they knew in their minds and hearts that the process towards creation relies on *risk*, *daring* and *courage*. This knowledge manifested itself in *sensory* and *kinaesthetic* (physical) connections. For them, it was the vital foundation for the acting journey. Their bodies became vessels from which their spirits were able to take flight. These Russian actors were impassioned and totally committed. It was an absolute joy to work with them. They demonstrated such clarity, inner concentration, and a vigorous freedom of expression. They knew that all of their painstaking, back-breaking, mechanical and technical classes would produce *skills*, which would release and support their creativity, and without this work, their inspiration would be flawed.

Many of the exercises in this book were workshopped in that class. The actors' excitement grew as they could feel the energy associated with the exercises begin to effect their muscles. I believe that it is at *this* level that deep learning takes place. Ultimately, these actors had been taught (or had been allowed to learn) that instinct and intuition, once given permission, will lead to authentic personal creation.

How then can we activate this permission? Where does it reside?

The Creative State

It has been said that the acting craft can be separated into three main elements: *intuition*, *imagination*, *common sense*. To me these elements represent the following:

Intuition is often called the actor's 'hunch'; the instinct within that provides the actor with creative impulses born of his or her inner, unspoken knowledge. It can vary in response to the material you work on. Your intuitive connections may sometimes be fierce, yet at other times this inner knowledge eludes you and you must look elsewhere to support your creative drive.

Common sense concerns itself with what is known, or the facts. For example, your craft and technical knowledge may offer logical solutions to any acting demand. This is guided by what you believe or know to be the playwright's intentions. Common sense enables you to employ any element of technique which you believe will help in the achievement of your acting goal.

Imagination encompasses your appetite for all that is possible. In this interior 'dream state' you allow yourself the licence to explore each idea with an unlimited scope. Logical boundaries, preconceived parameters and the sense of the appropriate, desert you. You find yourself dissolving the lifeline to the 'parent ship' and, with courage and naivety, following your fantasy.

It is in *this* state that your inner critic is set aside. The fax in your head awaiting reception lies idle. The usual incoming messages — *You cannot do this... It can't be done... You're going to be wrong... What you're attempting is not within your range...Give up now before you're worthlessness becomes too evident... Stick to what you know... stay safe, otherwise, you'll only get hurt* — these commands do not compute. You find no program with which to access them. But inwardly you observe one lone signal, gently blinking: *I'm right with you... where shall we go?*

At these moments everything seems easy. Any challenge empowers you. Your child-like innocence and playfulness runs in tandem with your extraordinary wealth of human experience and, out of this, you begin to actualise your potential. Without attempting to be original, *this* is where your uniqueness resides.

Concepts Made Concrete

Much of my teaching has been an exploration and indeed affirmation of the actor's 'creative state'. I have, with my actors, continued to discover how this state may be induced and what obstacles emerge to thwart it. Through various structures used as launching pads, it has been our aim to activate the physical radiation of one's *aliveness*, hence allowing the pure, unadulterated release of the actor's *free child*, where the creative spirit resides.

All of the exercises are aimed at getting the focus off you and onto the other actor and your shared moment-by-moment stage life. They are about *activation:* igniting the actor's *interior fire*; making active all the dynamics you will require on the rehearsal room floor and in performance — aliveness, receptivity, communication, contact, the here and now, passion, courage, versatility, open channels, inventiveness, surrender, vulnerability, joy, power, alertness, sensory awareness — in essence, activating the creative, authentic self.

There is one aspect of my work which I actually call 'Creative State'. These classes are usually non-verbal and involve the entire class for the duration of the session. They are mostly highly energetic and eccentric, but are sometimes simple, subtle and internalised. They can be extremely rhythmic, patterned and conceptual, but they always release and support the actor's imagination and creative drive. For a product is never sought, a judgment never made.

As a result the actors feel affirmed and any blocks or barriers often seem less permanent, for the class jettisons the actor into a world where he or she can be at one with his or her creativity and unique outlook. As such, this class becomes a 'touchstone' to each individual's sense of self and the reason he or she creates. So often drama schools focus primarily on the *success* of actors in their current production rather than on *preparing* them for their future creative lives. This lethal cocktail of 'success' mixed with 'correctness' can lead to what I call the see-I-can-do-it style of acting, which reduces creative evolution to mere pushing, proving and attaining.

Interestingly, during my first year at the Western Australian Academy of Performing Arts, I came across a book detailing the work of Michael Chekhov, a great Russian actor and teacher. He worked closely with Stanislavsky at the Moscow Art Theatre for over sixteen years and then worked around the world. Migrating to America in 1927, he established his revolutionary and much acclaimed acting studio as well as various theatre companies. He integrated the inner truth and emotional depth of Stanislavsky's system with his own sense of awakening the actor's spirit and intuition. His beliefs continued to evolve as he worked as an actor and director until his death in 1955.

In *Lessons for the Professional Actor* released in 1985, Mel Gordon's introduction states:

> Chekhov made actor-training fun. The internal censors that prevent many actors from attempting untried ideas and roles — 'not to appear stupid or ridiculous' — cease to function normally when the work is framed in a non-adult, or risk-free manner. Chekhov also created blocks of exercises that produced a rush of exhilaration or energy in his students. For Chekhov, the loss of mental energy or enthusiasm was one of the greatest obstacles to the creation of character, 'the sense of aliveness on stage'.

Coincidentally, my approach has developed along acutely similar lines: once an actor *believes* and his or her inner confidence grows, the creative state is produced. For an actor can only do something onstage if they *believe* they can. When this belief is married to an alert and heightened receptivity to the entire stage picture which surrounds them, then true shared invention becomes possible. The concept of art being a communal activity becomes a reality.

The Power Within

I remember an exhilarating class taught by the American voice specialist Rowena Balos. In this hurried lunchtime workshop, Rowena faced over sixty students from various courses and a dozen teachers, all of whom wanted to observe and take notes. But it was not to be: this was a sensory workshop. The knowledge gained was 'of the body' and would therefore be more significant in its lasting impact.

As we stood awkwardly, scattered across the rehearsal floor awaiting the commencement of the class, the room was charged with inhibition and embarrassment. A frenetic tension possessed each participant as we wondered what may be 'required' of us. Our focus was firmly anchored on what we stood to *lose*.

One of the first exercises was for all of us to stand with some space around us. Our script was, 'I am scared', and the physical movement, a sharp step *back*. After repeating this four or five times, we were asked again to repeat the line but *this* time, to step *forward.*

Why, after this exercise, was the entire room ready to freely experience all the class had to offer? Firstly, because we had acknowledged our fear and secondly, because we now stepped forward, we had replaced the unsaid word at the end of the line, 'I am scared **so** *(...I'll hold back, protect myself, stay safe)*, with 'I am scared **and** *(...I'll give it a go, risk, dare to learn).*

In this state of creative openness we believe risk is rewarding, for it means growth. We know it doesn't matter *what* may happen — our focus rests securely on committing to the *process.* When this state is achieved with actors, all is indeed possible.

The next phase in Rowena's class was to step forward and replace the words 'I am scared' with 'I am powerful'! This caused a mild earth tremor when suggested. Not just 'I am scared and... *I'll give it a go'*, but 'and... *I will be powerful within my creation*'. Interestingly enough, this proved a far more confronting task for the teachers than for the students. But slowly, each participant in their own way and in their own time, publicly stated there was potential for powerful creativity within them. From this point, the true process could begin.

We all know we are the source of our own creativity, our own expression. We need to be reminded and indeed encouraged to embrace that responsibility *and* open ourselves to all its possibilities.

So, to recap: '...it is from this spontaneous toying and exploration that there arises the hunch, the creative seeing of life in a new and significant way...'.

The rehearsal exercises ahead present many opportunities where you can toy with the possibilities of your *speech* and juggle *its* various elements. We will work towards unplugging from what we feel is correct and expected and surrender to our authentic connection to the purity of the work.

Chapter 3

The Basis of Craft

Pack it Up, Ship it Out

When we begin preparing for our audition, we often cannot help thinking about the presentation — we see the *form* which it might take. And why not? We want to be sure it will be perceived as legitimate and believable thereby validating our abilities.

Because we seek this validation, the first departure we often make from embracing the material in a pure way is to focus on two *end* products — *character* and *emotion*. We feel we must have these two elements alive and kicking if we're to have a chance. We imagine that if we enter these dynamic regions early in our rehearsal period we'll be truly involved and studiously *working*.

Therefore we begin involving ourselves with the package which surrounds the piece: the conditions, the state, the feelings, the sensations, how it should sound, how it should look, how it should *feel* being this other person. We are working toward *product* — towards an end result. Without adequate time spent deciphering *what* the material consists of — its structure and components — we focus on *how* it may be performed and presented. In other words, rather than *penetrating* the character's thinking, we begin to *impose* final solutions.

The danger with this approach is that it can lead to the trap discussed in Chapter One: *imitation*, that is, what you feel will be most *appropriate.* So many auditions have inadvertently foundered because of this initial approach of simply trying *too* hard *too* soon to *make it work, to get it right.*

To redress this emphasis on 'solutions' we will begin by focusing on the first stages of the process, then look at ways of channelling our creative power.

The Search for Truth

Firstly, Robert Benedetti says: 'character and emotion are not the *precursor* of action, they are the *result* of action'. In other words, you do not have to activate these two elements to produce 'drama'. Drama springs from what happens — the events that take place, the 'action'. If in your rehearsals you *experience* this action (Stanislavsky's *score*), you will not be able to *avoid* experiencing character and emotion. They become by-products of your commitment to and fulfilment of, the scene's action.

For example, stand quite neutrally in your room with some space around you. Your script is still 'I'm scared'. Without thinking of 'how' you could say the line, or what emotion may be applicable, simply state the line whilst taking one step backwards. After doing this a couple of times, make this small adjustment: Step back a little *sharper* and with more *speed*. Whilst repeating this a few times, allow yourself to access any sensations or impulses that surface. You should sense an emotional connection beginning. Without thinking of how you *feel* or indeed *who* you are, this knowledge begins to emerge.

Now raise your arm as if you were pointing to someone. Your line is 'Stop right there'. Repeat this gesture and line three or four times. Now take a sharp step *forward* whilst swiftly raising your arm. Repeat this three or four times. Once again, the action begins to induce an attitude to what you are doing (who you are — character) and also leads to the text becoming motivated (how you feel — emotion).

The above examples are simple but hold an essential truth: Committing to the action of the scene leads to the emergence of a stronger and purer reality; working for end results can significantly retard the process towards that truth.

Looking at the greater picture for a moment, suppose your character breakdown reads: 'Bitter Old Lag'. You can't act a label, and playing a characteristic results in repetition and consistency — both hallmarks of dull acting. So what internal reasons and motivations drive the action which will *produce* this label of 'bitterness'? Through your rehearsal period you will begin to uncover the true cause — you will understand that this character is a *frustrated traditionalist.* This is the cause which results in the worldly appearance of bitterness which manifests itself in many ways and forms. The character's acute desire to have the world around them burn, given the zeal they feel for tradition, standards and principles, leads them to be constantly insulted and abused because the new world in which they find themselves thinks differently. Their actions reflect this tension: they berate, scold, contradict, defend and dismiss — bitter actions indeed.

The next role you audition for or play is labelled 'Angry Bully'. Through your internal investigation you once again form a relationship with the inner cause. Beyond the character's public persona of anger and hostility you see the *lonely, isolated searcher*. You then ensure that this is reflected in the detail of the character's exchanges — they agitate, inflame, provoke, patronise, refute and intimidate. Their anger and attitude of dominance towards all around them prevails; loneliness and isolation is set firmly within.

And so the process continues. The 'stupid eccentric' who is seen as ludicrous and often irritating, is fuelled by the *excited obsessive* within. Their actions are to demand, scrutinise, engross, indoctrinate, enthral, outsmart. They see themselves as a *visionary*, but their possessive and pedantic nature creates another impression altogether. The 'unpleasant spinster' becomes the *injured loner*, demanding emotional compensation and seeking personal validity though reproaching, demeaning and disenchanting.

When the italics supplied by the playwright before the line read '*Hysterical*', you connect to the inner stimulus which you discover to be absolute *fear*, which causes the outward signs called 'hysteria'. When the character '*violently lashes out*' you incorporate into your internal landscape the stark, all-encompassing *terror* which grips the character. The driving internal cause is revealed through *action* which then produces an effect.

Sound and Fury Signifying Nothing

The term 'effects' can sometimes be deadly, so easily luring actors into a contrived and false world. Take, for example, the following stage directions or 'effects' which George Bernard Shaw offers his actors in the play *Saint Joan*. These are all presented by Shaw as a reference to *how* the line is to be interpreted and then played. They are intended as *helpers* or *pointers* to playing the moment successfully:

- *interposing smoothly*
- *rising impetuously*
- *with a not too friendly smile*
- *playing the pink of courtesy*
- *furiously disappointed*
- *flushing angrily*
- *in a blaze of courage*
- *unabashed and rather roughly*

- *with a mixture of cynical admiration and contempt*
- *distressed, but incapable of seeing the effect she is producing*
- *rising, with a flush of reckless happiness irradiating her face.*

How easy it would be to simply embrace this end result and efficiently produce the desired theatrical effect. And how easy then for the audience's attention to be steadfastly fixed not upon the character's *situation*, but on the actor's *success* at achieving the form. The *effect* only draws attention to the form — the *cause* brings the audience towards true understanding and involvement.

Many playwrights and many, *many,* directors communicate their ideas and desires by describing the 'shell' which encases the effect they wish to create, i.e. look angrier, get sexier, be funnier *etc.* Actors must then decode or deconstruct the direction and find a justifiable and organic way of connecting to the *cause* which will *produce* the correct end result. Let's look more closely at another moment from *Saint Joan*. In Act One, Scene 2 Joan pleads her case to the Dauphin. She attempts to convince him to fight the English until they are banished from all of France and he is consecrated and crowned. He replies: 'I cannot do it. I am not built that way; and there is an end to it'. Shaw gives Joan's next line as: 'Blethers! We are all like that to begin with. I shall put courage into thee'.

The italics preceding her line read 'trenchant and masterful'. How are you then to say the line? Trenchantly and with great mastery, I suppose. Let's decode Shaw's instruction: 'Trenchant' can mean cutting, vigorous or scathing; 'masterful' can mean qualified or authoritative. Before we attach Joan's attitude to the exchange, let's look at her stimulus — the *cause.*

Charles' weak nature and pathetic inability to take responsibility make him totally dismissive of Joan's plea, replying: '... And there's an end to it'. Joan, however, vigorously denies his attitude through her action to *berate*: 'Blethers! We are all like that to begin with'. She then calls upon her defiant inner strength and knowledge and *empowers* him: 'I shall put courage into thee'. Her attitude when she berates him is self-assured, confident, full of *vigour*. And when she plays the action to empower, her steely and impassioned sense of right and absolute *authority* is harnessed.

Only then, through this inner process, will a trenchant and masterful manner be apparent and serve the play in the way Shaw intended.

You must always find the essential *essence* of any image or effect you need to inhabit — otherwise the image will not work. The 'angry' person may be found to be insecure; the 'hopeless' victim may be uncloaked to discover loneliness. The characters' actions need to spring from this integrated source, and through their *action*s we determine how others perceive them and the emotions which ensue.

Therefore, take your focus off *finding* a character and *creating* emotional states and commit firstly to what lies on the page: the facts, the action. Fulfil these requirements first and allow the rest to follow. This will lead to a connected and centred approach where you are open to the potential and the truth of the piece.

Don't Try, Allow

I was teaching a workshop at the University of California, San Diego a number of years ago. During the class we were doing a warm-up exercise called 'circle offers'. How this works is that in a circle of actors, one actor walks across the circle towards another. That actor says a line and makes some physical contact. The receiver doesn't respond verbally, but simply accepts the offer. He/she then moves across the circle to approach another actor with a *new* offer. This proceeds until all the actors have made and received various offers.

The focus of the exercise is on the actor as both receiver and transmitter; the two fundamental aspects of acting. These two dynamics must be honed and active in performance so the stage action can flow through each actor and create cause and effect. In other words, through our sensory reception we accept each stimulus; it makes its imprint upon our emotions and we therefore react, affecting someone else in turn. This process drives the play and directs its journey.

The 'circle offers' exercise allows each actor time to clearly *transmit* the offer in an effort to affect change within the listener. The *receiver* has time to simply accept the stimulus, without any concern to create a scene.

One actor in our workshop chose the line 'I love you'. He approached another actor and proceeded to 'act out' the moment, which he filled to the brim with emotion and with a strong sense of 'character'. The offer was, inevitably, swamped by emotion. The receiver wasn't affected because the actor had essentially had much more effect upon *himself*, because that was where his focus lay. He believed that if *he* could feel and experience the offer (the love), then it must be real. The only information we, as the audience, received through this moment was what *mood* the character was experiencing. In dramatic terms, this is an inactive choice as it doesn't produce *action* — it doesn't develop the dramatic situation. Onstage, every moment must be a movement into the *future* .

After asking him to repeat the offer more simply and to allow more *contact* — *trusting* the action through the physical gesture — the actor realised what was needed. But his search led him *further* within. He so desperately wanted to 'be' someone in an effort to produce 'the moment', the desired effect, that he began squeezing the text for meaning; he stammered the line; and his physical gestures towards the receiver were tense. After a dozen attempts, and with his frustration building, we tried something else.

I asked him to stand neutrally and to look clearly at the other actor's face — her eyes, lips — to see the offer within *her* rather than within *himself* — to allow his senses to *receive* the stimulus before him. Then, I asked him to simply commit to the physical gesture of touch: to allow this to guide him and to become his focus; to trust the *action*. Once this connection was made and he relinquished his mental grip on the form, his fingers became his release mechanism. Consequently, the sensory association triggered by this action led him and informed all he did. The line then flowed with such ease and clarity, affecting the receiver and creating a very intimate and powerful moment between them. The choice became *active*; the play moved forward.

The actor had discovered he didn't need to *supply* the scene with emotion, that the scene could create circumstances where the emotion became *unavoidable*. By accepting the other actor as the stimulus and then committing to the action, his *reaction* released him. Any sense of 'imitation' left him, and a pure, personal impulse was forged.

The Actor's Score

How do you go about uncovering the action? In life, as you know, we have a series of needs, moment by moment, which need fulfilling. We go about getting what we want through a series of physical *and* psychological actions. But often we are thwarted: obstacles emerge, either internally or externally, and we adjust our tactics and/or change objectives accordingly.

Stanislavsky called this our 'score' — as in a musical score. But, as opposed to *musical* notations which depict tempo, key, style and so on, our daily score depicts *thoughts, emotions* and *actions.* The character's score, which the actor must discover and plot during rehearsals, involves the same: a sequence of objectives revealed through physical and psychological expression.

Rehearsals are about uncovering the score of this expression, which will dynamically serve the actor's interpretation. This should enable the story you intend to tell being articulated via the play's *action*. Playwrights write plays and therefore words, not to be read, but *acted* — to be revealed through *action*. The script is merely the blueprint of this action. If you find the right action through discovering the *score*, the words simply flow.

> Conscious activity in preparing and rehearsing a role needed to be coherent and so organised as to create the conditions in which spontaneous, intuitive creation could occur... this is the sole purpose of *the system.*[9]

In the exercises that follow, we will study a number of speeches and reveal each scene's action to form our initial foundation. Once this important preparation work has been embraced the conditions are set for our next stage — creative exploration.

Chapter 4

Activating the Physical

Point of Concentration

In order to gain maximum benefit from your creative investigation, you need a secure point of focus for your energies.

The actor's 'point of concentration' offers three essential elements:

1. It focuses your energy.
2. It directs your concentration.
3. It gives you an aim to all you do on stage[10]

At an audition there are any number of points of concentration upon which you may focus before the approaching event. Two of the most popular are: 'I've *got* to get this job' and 'I'll *never* get this job'. As you will have no doubt experienced, concentrating on either of these can fuel self-consciousness and breed failure. However, you could trust in your preparation, and devote your entire energies to *'I want to present the emotional life of my character'*. This is the most positive, *practical,* and promising point of concentration.

How you go about *hosting* your own audition in this way requires thought and exploration. In the rehearsal of your piece your job is to pick the right point of concentration — the one which will activate and release you into the action — for each *moment* onstage. Once again, I am talking about the actor's *score*. Once plotted, the audition becomes about the *doing*, not the self-conscious *being.* In other words, you don't re-create the *form* in the hope of it being liked and accepted, but you re-inhabit the *structure* and lose yourself in the *doing.* As Stanislavsky said, if the body feels, the soul will respond. If you have mapped out the physical and psychological action of the scene, through committing to each of these moments, the emotional life will present itself and backup all you do and say. Many actors think they have to feel it before they can say it. However, you can also feel it *because* you say it. Trust that the words will lead you to the experience for they are the residue of that experience.

What emerges from this approach? The full embodiment and release of the character's emotional life. And what were your auditioners hoping to witness during your all too brief time with them? Precisely that.

> Your point of concentration is your springboard into the intuitive — it allows *perceiving* rather than *preconception* to occur.[12]

Once again, we are searching for approaches which will alleviate or indeed vanquish any sense of self-consciousness — the actor's major debilitator. Once you become overly aware of *how* what you are doing is being perceived, self-monitoring begins. You begin to judge your 'effects'. You cease to trust your organic and intuitive connections and an analytical and calculated mind-set takes over.

The camera which usually resides within, seeing what you see, suddenly becomes mobile. It tracks outside of you and then pans back, trapping you in its intense and critical glare. Under this harsh, unforgiving focus you seem to have little choice but to monitor and edit all you do and say, seeing yourself objectively and larger than life — a 70mm, Dolby sound play-back, running constantly and relentlessly through your head.

You continue acting however, remembering lines and moves, looking as competent as you can and working with your usual exterior efficiency and charm. But all the while an internal gladiatorial clash rages between two enemies — your creative connection versus your chief judge, censor and executioner. As an actor, you know who often wins.

Under these conditions, how can one expect to communicate effectively, reveal the authentic self and engage in any sort of fulfilling creative release?

One way I try to help actors when this occurs in an audition, is to re-connect them to their *physical lives*. Because our body-sense is so strong it only needs a small trigger to enable it to shed its imitation and re-engage its inner knowledge. It is sometimes suggested to actors that their speech be done in conjunction with a vital physical activity, such as playing racquet ball, squash, or shadow boxing. Often this physical focus relieves their speech of its vice-like pattern which the actor has imposed and a spontaneous 'aliveness' ensues. Often the sense becomes clearer, as the actor begins to *physically* inhabit the character's inner workings — receiving stimulus, processing its meaning, and then releasing a new energy based on the character's needs. When this begins to take place, self-consciousness departs, for it cannot be accommodated within these inner processes.

Obviously every speech cannot be staged by using a sport theme or intense activity, but the work we'll do shortly will be as vital, as physical, and as releasing. In these exercises we will choose specific points of concentration to help you to actualise your potential and discover the full experience your piece can offer.

After these intrinsic and organic connections have been forged, your camera will remain locked, unable to move. In your audition, when you feel stressed, under pressure and exposed, your full energy will flow freely into your creative invention.

As Lawrence Olivier said, the golden rule of acting is 'know exactly what you're going to do, *and then do it*'.

The Unknown Factor

One major cause of self-consciousness is that many actors, while performing their speech, try and second-guess what the auditioners are looking for. They voluntarily monitor each moment of their performance, adjusting any aspect of it if they sense this adjustment might be perceived as being more 'suitable'. So much energy expended on a false focus.

Ninety-nine times out of one hundred, you will *never* know what your auditioners are thinking or indeed what they want. *They* may not even know at this stage of their project. As soon as you walk in they may look at your height or hair colour and know casting you is, for whatever reason, impractical. To you, they now seem slightly disinterested, or worse still, *over-polite*. They offer you less time than the previous actor and tell you less about the project than you heard they would. This begins to rob you, second by painful second, of your belief in what you had prepared.

All you can do is act, according to what you know — based on the character/script/project — however inconclusive these facts may be. Then, with full empowerment, you must rest your point of concentration firmly on presenting the emotional life of the role as you see it, with the decisions as you have made them.

Of course you may be totally wrong in your interpretation. Given the scarcity of facts about the project and the absence of a complete script to read, you may have had to rely mostly on your imagination and sense of invention. If this is the case, then so be it.

Zan Sawyer-Daily, casting director for the Actor's Theatre of Louisville, told of an audition she witnessed where an actor came in to read for a new play. The audition scene sent out was one between a mother and her son. The actor's audition script however, only read 'WOMAN 1' and 'MAN 1'. Based on his feelings toward the scene, the actor concluded that the two characters were passionate lovers experiencing a tumultuous rift in their relationship. He arrived for his appointment, met all concerned with the project, and prepared to begin his audition. The *older* woman who had been hired to read opposite each person auditioning took her place on the set. The actor began his audition. He worked very well off the other actor: his choices all reflecting his belief about their turbulent relationship; his actions and gestures all informed by the dilemma in which he and his lover had found themselves. With a physical familiarity and assuredness, he touched, kissed and caressed his way through the scene, producing an acute intimacy between them and also revealing a deep emotional estrangement.

At the conclusion of the audition, the artistic director, casting director, producer, author and also the mature and very experienced other actor, sat looking toward the young actor, shocked and speechless. After some discussion, the mix-up eventually revealed itself. The actor had committed so completely to his interpretation, however, that he was offered the job — not only because of his obvious talent and preparedness, but also because his version of the scene had inspired the director to consider another dimension to the mother/son relationship previously unthought of.

This was, of course, a lucky coincidence, but the example still holds truth. What you present in your audition must be fully inhabited and fully crafted. It will then be clear that the package you present has been thoroughly worked through and conceived. If your *interpretation* was not what the auditioners were after, you'll have given them an opportunity to re-align your obvious talent into a different form. If *you* are not what they're after, they'll keep you in mind for the future. Why wouldn't they remember a solid, well-prepared, committed actor who cares about their work?

The House is Now Live

We have spoken of *your* point of concentration, but what are the *auditioner's* and *audience's* points of concentration? Before they focus on whether they like or dislike what they're viewing; if they feel it is appropriate or not; if they agree with the acting or it isn't what they were expecting; their *first* focus falls quite simply on, 'Do I *believe* this reality?'

And how will they perceive this reality or lack thereof? Through your *physical life*. Even if the *sound* of what you're doing seems real, their *visual* perception is where their belief firmly rests.

The Body Speaks

Everything your body says (and it won't lie) the audience will take in, digest, and make decisions upon. Therefore, you'd better be absolutely sure your body is registering exactly what you want the audience to receive. Tension, nerves, lack of preparation, running on adrenalin, hoping to 'please', wanting to 'impress' — these things will be physically manifest and take the auditioner's or audience's focus *off* the character and onto *you*.

To counteract this, be sure your rehearsal work *physically connects* you to the action, language, needs and images inherent in the piece, to your onstage environment and to those with whom you are interacting (imaginary or actual).

> Reality can only be physical, in that it is received and transmitted through the sensory equipment. Through physical relationships all life onstage springs.[12]

In the rehearsal process we know that the intellect can inhibit and the emotions, being only states, are not the best points from which to begin your journey. Where then can you begin the exploration of your role? With what is most immediately available, with what responds most easily — your body.

> An actor on the stage need only sense the smallest modicum of organic *physical* truth in his action or general state and instantly his emotions will respond to his inner faith and genuineness of what his body is doing. In our case it is incomparably easier to call forth real truth and faith within the region of our physical than of our spiritual nature. An actor need only believe in himself and his soul will open up to receive all the inner objectives and emotions of his role.[13]

The actor is a vessel into which another life pours — with different emotions, ideals and ways of dealing with the world. As actors you are conduits through which this new energy flows. You must allow these changes to affect you *physically,* for once your body feels, your soul will respond. As we discovered in Chapter Two, physical triggers activate emotional connections. To enable this to happen you must surrender to the circumstances around you and allow them to be the physical guide with which you start your journey into your new reality — the world of the play.

Improvising, whether verbal or non-verbal, can be a tremendous vehicle for this work, as it is a spontaneous, personal, instinctive response to a given stimulus or circumstance. It can personalise a situation or a moment for an actor instantaneously, at once fusing intellectual understanding with *sensation.*

Concepts are useless to actors unless they become *experiences.* Our minds can be cold, rational, logical and analytical. By intellectualising the experience, we can deaden our senses. The more we engage *physically*, the more our senses become alert and enlivened, therefore creating the possibility for powerful experiences. If our minds decrease the potency of the work, our bodies must become the antidote.

The exercises in this book have been designed for this specific purpose: to enable you to inhabit and be transformed by the dynamics of your scene. This will then forge a close relationship between all you do, say and feel, enabling this essential belief to be palpable for yourself and, of course, your audience.

Chapter 5

An Empty Stage at the Service of Invention [14]

Your exploration work on your chosen piece can and should be exciting. Getting a piece together for an audition presents a chance to work your craft and the actual audition presents the opportunity to *perform.* Embrace these opportunities as a part of your ongoing process as an actor. Every screen test, audition *and* interview presents moments where you 'do' your art. Seize them and enjoy!

Different processes and exercises trigger different responses in actors. The exercises in PART TWO of this book present an array of possibilities. But before we move on to the exercises, I would like to explain where my particular approach stems from. The class illustrated below consists of a series of exercises designed principally for scene work. These will give you a good indication of the potential of this approach when it comes to your solo monologue and will help to propel you imaginatively into the world of your scene.

Many of the exercises contained in this book were developed during a block of scene work I was teaching at The National Institute of Dramatic Art (NIDA) in Sydney during 1988. We had already had much input into the left side of our brains where data and information storage is processed and retained. This is always necessary during certain stages of training. But I felt it important at this time, and with this group of actors, to activate the right side of their brains where intuition, instinct and fantasy reside.

The Journey — Fact-finding

Firstly, after choosing their scenes and partners, the actors read the scenes to the class for *sense*. This was to be the foundation of all that would follow: Not how do I *feel* about what I'm saying, but what do I want to make *understood* as a *result* of what I am saying.

Finding the sense and establishing the meaning are two very distinct stages of this preliminary work. Discovering the *meaning* requires an emotional attachment which springs from the character's specific inner monologue and point of view at that instant. It also comes from the *physical sensations* which occur during the exchange. These you can discover on the rehearsal room floor. It is too soon at this stage to start supplying emotions and attaching them to the text. Spend time searching for the *sense* — the linear knowledge of *what* is being said, rather than *how* it is being said. Own and inhabit the thoughts which the character is communicating. In other words, avoid final solutions and penetrate the character's thinking process.

This naturally led us into discussing the action, that is, what happens in the scene, what events take place. We then asked how these events are affected by the context of the play: i.e. What do they offer the play? How do they move the play and its themes forward? What would the play lose if the scene was to be cut?

This is an excellent way of pinpointing function. The actor's fundamental question should be: 'How does this scene contribute to the reason why the play was written?' Indeed, how does every *moment* of my performance contribute? Robert Benedetti often speaks of this as a sure fire way for the actor to be able to identify why the scene is integral to the play and what responsibilities the actor has in facilitating the telling of the story.

We then looked at the general *beats* within the scene (see EXERCISE 2). That is, when the focus of the scene changed radically, or when a character's wants altered sufficiently for the scene to change course as a result. We noted any *atmospheric* changes — where temperature or any other outside stimulus affected the mood of the scene. This ultimately helped to reveal the main events and any crisis which led to an event.

That was our preparation stage. It allowed us to acknowledge *what* was on the page in terms of language, plot, action and the playwright's structure. *How* we were to perform it and *why* the characters said what they did, were not discussed. But through this work the actors became very familiar with the lines (as the scenes were quite short), which enabled us to move easily to the next stage of the process.

A Secure World

Each pair then built a *four-walled environment* in which their scene could exist, for example, the lounge, the caravan, the boardroom. It was four-walled because I wanted the actor's focus to be entirely on their scene partner and the interaction within their environment. I wanted to take away the need to 'present' or 'perform' the scene and 'play it out front'. It was to be an intimate and private exchange between the characters without them thinking at all of the audience. This was a rehearsal, not a performance, and the experience for the actor was to be one of *being*, not *proving.*

The centre of the rehearsal room was claimed as a 'timeless' and 'placeless' region — a 'twilight zone' where the raw dynamics, truths and issues of the scene, could be explored and battled out free from naturalism, circumstantial restraints and appropriateness. It was a blank canvas where the characters' inner worlds, emotional lives and potentials could be experienced and released to the full.

The actors were free at any time to depart to this arena, to instinctively follow an impulse, to discover a depth or quality within the scene and to pursue it, then take it back onto their 'set' and allow it to affect and inform the scene and its atmosphere.

Extending the Boundaries

Some of the 'departures' offered to the actors to explore in this twilight zone were:

- Without words, transform the scene's journey into *heightened movement,* culminating in the main event of the scene at the end of one minute.
- Sum up your character's major 'want' *in one word.* Using this word and that of your partner's, improvise and battle the two issues against one another. That is, control *vs* independence, power *vs* respect, indulgence *vs* abstinence, revenge *vs* honour.
- Sit back-to-back with your partner and begin the scene, simply contacting each of the ideas. After each line, take turns with your partner to say, *'And again'*. The line is then repeated until the *idea* behind it is revealed clearly. You may say *'And again'* three of four times per line.
- Lie on the ground facing your partner. Cover your scripts with one hand. Then uncover your scripts line by line and communicate each thought to each other through *eye contact* only. Observe major punctuation, i.e. **? . !**
- Experience the journey of the scene using only *one word* from each line. Choose a word which carries the essence of the line.
- Take any beat from the scene and *explore and heighten*: the love; the humour; the conflict; the discoveries (see EXERCISE 3).

• Stand back-to-back and say each line accompanied by a *heightened physical action* which sums up the idea or thought behind it.

• Do the scene, prefacing each line with *'And then he/she decides to say...'*. This clarifies the character's choice and reminds you to enter their moment-by-moment thought process.

• Do the scene, making *physical contact* on every line, no matter how fleeting. Repeat this, avoiding touching the arms of the other person. Repeat again, this time avoiding using your hands as the means of contact.

• As you move around the space, explore without the use of speech the *physical relationship* and *dynamics of the characters' interaction*. For example, who is the hunter and who the prey? Who is the visionary and who the follower? Who holds the status and power physically, emotionally? When does it change? How? What does each character stand to gain or lose from the other?

• Choose *four issues* the character is fighting for. For example, love, honour, repentance, deception, forgiveness, betrayal. Improvise using your four words and those of your partner. Allow the issues to clash as you pursue your needs.

• Do the scene *without words*, exploring the journey of the scene, beat by beat, through eye contact only.

• Move around the space. *Freeze* every five seconds, exploring some aspect of your relationship to the other character. Use distance, closeness, levels and heights and gestures. Fill the space, ensuring that throughout the exercise you reveal the variety of needs alive and at work within the relationship.

• *Swap characters* in the scene.

• Without words, *contact the environment,* the surrounding *atmosphere* and your partner's *presence*. Experience this atmosphere in which the scene resides and springs from, without drama or acting. Feel the air around you become charged.

• After you say your line, *mumble your inner monologue* aloud under your partner's line. This should propel and fuel your next line and exchange (see EXERCISE 4).

• After each of your partner's lines, ask out loud, *'Is this good or bad for me?'* Then quickly process his or her offer, decide how you feel, and allow that information to inform your next choice and subsequent line (see EXERCISE 5).

• After exploring the scene's journey through heightened movement, choose *three physically repeatable motifs* which sum up or embrace your character's needs. One must involve your legs, one your arms, and one your torso. Improvise with your partner using these motifs.

• Repeat the exercise above, now using both *your* three movements *and* those of your partner. You may use his or her motifs to question them or taunt them.

• After each line, *mumble your need.* For example: 'Come here now.' (*I can't bear to be alone!*) 'Why should I believe you?' (*He's losing ground — pursue him)* (see EXERCISE 7).

• Whilst moving, and in your own time, explore your character's *personal space-* the space around them which they deem to be their property, it may be three inches or twelve feet. Define this space, then *double* it. Find the degree of space most appropriate for your character. Now decide how the character *affects this air* around him or her as he or she moves: Is the air heavy and pushed? Light and floating? Erratic, dangerous, sharp? *Double* its dynamic, explore the sensations, then allow it to become more subtle. But first, push the boundaries.

• Decide on the character's energy centre: is it the head, the heart or gut, where the energy is mostly centred? Double its speed and force. Be driven and consumed by this motor. Allow these dynamic changes to inform the character's inner life so to heighten the experience of 'living' your character.

• Along with your partner, choose a line each from the scene and *explore your relationship* through that line whilst moving around the space. Explore the exchange through speed, the distance between you, levels and heights.

• Whilst moving around the space, accentuate the characters' *public persona* or image presented to the other. Claim it, embody it, exaggerate it. Then, release its *private* self — the one they shield from the other. Embody it, explore its energy and hidden needs. With your partner, snap in and out of these two worlds and inhabit both sets of dynamics. Experience any tension between the two.

• Whilst walking around, contemplate the character's *ultimate fantasy ending* to the scene. Regardless of whether it happens or not, or *could* ever happen, choose the ultimate climax to the scene. Run to a private part of the room, and spend ten seconds by yourself living this ending. *Experience* the murder, the sacrifice, the love, the redemption, the betrayal or the ecstasy.

• Stand six metres from your partner. See a part of their character you want to touch — a part you love, cherish, respect, are turned-on by. Take thirty seconds to walk towards your partner, preparing to touch and embrace that part. Stop at twenty-nine seconds and a few centimetres from an actual touch. Allow this quality of your partner's to 'imprint' upon your entire body during your journey towards him or her.

• Repeat the exercise as above, but choose a part of your partner's character you despise or resent, a part you'd like to tear or smash or by which you are frightened. Take thirty seconds for the journey. Prepare your fist, feel the knife. Spend the last ten seconds preparing to follow through with your desired action in slow-motion. Stop at twenty-nine seconds and a breath away from the action.

• Walk around the space, keeping eye contact with your partner. See both of the qualities chosen above within him or her. Experience these *opposite dynamics* and allow them to affect the way you move through space and your non-verbal interchange.

And so the departures continued. All aimed to balance the work we had already done, with the *adventure* the scene has to offer. Some of the scenes I have worked on using the above approach have included May and Eddie from Shepard's *Fool For Love*, Francis and Betsheb from Nowra's *The Golden Age*, Trigorin and Arardina from Chekhov's *The Seagull*, Tom and Meg from Gow's *Away* and Barbara and Douglas in Gow's *Europe*, Platanov and Anna Petrovna from Chekhov's *Wild Honey*, Peter and Jerry from Albee's *Zoo Story*, and Leontes and Hermione from Shakespeare's *The Winter's Tale*.

It was quite amazing to witness the discoveries that were made in the free-wheeling, reckless 'zone' in the middle of the room, and to see how these discoveries ignited the interchange on the actor's return to their set. The scene became layered and took on a bold physicality, opposites were found, the actors embodied the language and released their energies with ease. The inner monologues became potent and fuelled the action. The actors began to want their partners not to *feel* what they were feeling, but to *understand* what they were saying. This is so very often a trap in acting — the need to emote. Lisle Jones often says, 'Acting is not about doing what you feel, but feeling what you have to do'.

Because of this clarity of thought the story became clear, the action defined, the choices and decisions sharp and specific. As a result the 'blocking' or physical life of the scene also took care of itself. If I was directing the scene I would now be in a position to work *reactively* from what was happening on the floor, as opposed to actively suggesting, motivating or 'moving' the scene because the actors were waiting to be told what to do.

This type of work can lend itself more appropriately to certain plays or scenes. Obviously the more physical and emotionally 'muscular', the better. But all drama needs to be extreme and profound no matter how subtly it may demand to be played, or how small the aperture through which you express it. For ultimately, subtlety is just a tightening of the focus in order to intensify.

These exercises are triggers to stimulate the most athletic responses to the character's interior landscape. Once experienced *physically*, they now reside within the character's range; they have been recorded on the character's tape or disk. How you wish to embody and *express* your character's needs now rests in your chosen interpretation and the terrain you wish to cover, given the vision of the production.

I have adapted the above work to aid your *solo* preparation and rehearsal of your audition speech. The exercises in PART TWO provide you with more specific ways to do this.

Damage Control

Sadly, the type of powerful and organic exploration outlined above, which is often the foundation work of many ensembles, is viewed cynically by many actors. They are either wary of its content and dubious of its results, or find the entire approach simply implausible.

Interestingly though, when these actors speak of their most remarkable audience experience to date, they mostly name the world's great ensembles. And what would be their fantasy future career? To be a part of a company whose work is based on the ensemble experience.

Why do actors seek this experience and imagine the opportunity will offer great nourishment? What creative sustenance will be digested to revitalise their souls? Why do they intuitively believe that vastly new and perhaps uncharted dimensions to their work will be ignited? The great luxury of 'time' is one reason. We often hear that a particular production was twelve months in the making and bemoan the fact we have but five weeks. We should note that often within that twelve-month period perhaps up to *five* different plays were being rehearsed. What else lies beneath our longing? For many, the ensemble embodies the artistic trilogy: the team, the trust, the process.

The Team, the Trust, the Process

These three magical elements combine to create an environment with *permission to play* at its core. The rehearsal *process* takes place in a creative arena where the *physical, organic,* inner connections to the world of the play and its characters are forged. Through a philosophical union of beliefs, the *team* affirms the journey ahead and produces a collective courage in all you undertake.

Then there's the other essential ingredient — the *trust*. I've often observed great productions and searched for how this ever-present trust manifests itself onstage. I believe it resides in the *rapport* between the players. A powerful and immediate *intimacy* underpins each moment. To my mind, this promotes a sensory and even *sensual* relationship between the play, the players and the audience. This unique energy creates a special experience and leads to that stage 'aura' we sometimes label atmosphere.

> Each performance should have an atmosphere which does not belong to anyone but belongs to the performance itself... the heartbeat... atmosphere gives us the air, the space around us. It coaxes our deeper feelings and emotions, our dreams... Without atmosphere we are imprisoned on the stage.[15]

With the team, trust and process, we, as actors, believe we at last can leave the world of imitation and uncover our unique creative voice. Due to time restraints, inadequate direction and insubstantial material, we are often forced into fabricating our acting in order to survive in our industry. Sadly, the audience has not only learnt to accept this fabrication but to *expect* it. As actors we believe the ensemble experience will release us and re-dress this lethal habit.

The Actor's Centre

One of the main reasons for my desire to establish The Actors' Centre in Sydney in 1987 was to offer an environment where true experimentation could take place — where, free from commercial pressures, actors could extend and expand their craft, re-evaluate and reinforce their skills and take those risks so essential to their continued creative development (*see* Plates 3 & 8). Now seven years old, we still search for new ways in which the Centre can be of benefit and how it may attract more members of the profession.

Fear holds many back from creative risk-taking. Fear of what? Are we scared of getting it wrong? What is 'it' anyway? What is this mythical 'correctness', hanging like a noose around our necks, strangling our creative courage and thwarting our sense of self?

In the Theatre De Complicité's production of *The Winter's Tale*, the company's director Simon McBurney was performing the role of Leontes. One of the most extraordinary scenes came in Act 3 when we discover that, because of his belief in Hermione's death, Leontes has chosen as his penance to crawl daily to the grave of his wife. In most productions this is accepted as a metaphorical statement. But here, it was *fact*. To see Leontes' bound and bloodied knees driving relentlessly into the earth, with the entire company also on their knees suffering the shame and bitterness by which he is consumed, was an immensely compelling theatrical statement.

Where did this choice come from? We can only imagine the actor gave himself the license to fall to the rehearsal room floor, remain there, and experiment with this potent physical impulse to see where it may lead. One second of self-doubt — 'Perhaps it won't work... What am I doing anyway? I might look stupid' — and the choice may never have found its way into the show's powerful landscape.

Indeed, without the entire company not only acknowledging but supporting his bold choice it may *not* have worked. But you will never know the extent of your creative ingenuity if you are not prepared to risk, then validate afterwards. If the idea doesn't work, drop it; if it serves your purpose, keep it, craft it, incorporate it.

Creative Independence

At the Academy, Lisle Jones often reminds the actors not to mistake 'the wish for the deed'. As a young actor in training I too used to wish with every fibre of my brain that I could make it work — somehow get it right. And I believed that if I was very, very lucky, and things perhaps fell into place, I might pull through and be cloaked in a reality deemed creative and believable. But my brain, the cold analytical computer, ruled my search, creating effort and contaminating almost every stage of the journey. In the rehearsal room, I was at the mercy of every silent opinion surrounding me. The worst, of course, being the toughest and most ruthless critic residing within. I was beginning to discover that if you don't act what you're compelled to act, then you act nothing.

But by changing my point of concentration from my actor's *fear* to the character's *beliefs*, effectively moving from my brain as the source of my motivation to my heart, 'deeds' began to replace the fruitless 'wishes' and I was able to unplug from my lethal mind-set based on luck, chance and fate. Rehearsals became a time of release, an *expedition* as opposed to a test of talent and validity. I had at last surrendered to the creative process, by allowing myself the permission, finally, to play.

In Sanskrit, the root of the verb 'to be' is 'to grow'.

The Next Step

So once again you need to remind yourself, 'I am scared, *and...*'. To help you to fully actualise your potential through your audition work, I offer the following opportunities. Hopefully through your experience of them you may even be able to say, 'I am *powerful, and...*'.

Each exercise is fully explained, its application described, your point of concentration outlined and various illustrations offered. They provide many exciting challenges and I'm sure they will prove stimulating for your work *beyond* the audition as well. The arena for creative risk-taking can extend from the audition to the rehearsal to the studio, and can include anyone who is also willing to break the boundaries of his or her creative expression. Commit to the adventure ahead. Best of luck!

PLATE 1
'Now't more outcastin...' Lisa Baumwol as Ayre in Louis Nowra's *The Golden Age,* directed by Dean Carey.

PLATE 2
'But all is not lost, oh no!' A scene from Ivan Turgenev's *A Month in the Country*, with Roxane Wilson as Natalia Petrovna. Directed by Dean Carey.

PLATE 3
Heidi Lapaine in the Actor's Centre presentation of *Lulu* by Franz Wedekind.

PLATE 4
'The ambition in my love thus plagues itself...' Jennifer Botica rehearses Helena from *All's Well That Ends Well.*

PLATE 5
'But now he's gone, and my idolatrous fancy must sanctify his relics.'
Again, Jennifer Botica rehearses Helena from *All's Well That Ends Well.*

PLATE 6
'I once told you, Marianne, you wouldn't escape my love...' John Adam and Deborah Galands in the final scene from Odon Von Horvath's *Tales From the Vienna Woods*. Directed by Dean Carey.

PART TWO

The Creative Arena

Rehearsal Room Exercises

EXERCISE 1: Extend/Advance

This exercise originated from Keith Johnstone's work at The Loose Moose Theatre Company in Calgary. It was designed to allow improvisers a way of enhancing any offers which emerged in a scene. An 'offer' can be an idea, a reaction, a suggestion, a decision — any major stimulus that affects the scene and the players.

Explanation Firstly, the exercise enabled the performers to acknowledge the offer which was to be focused upon, then it gave them time to extend and amplify the offer, which advanced the scene, in turn developing the action.

The idea was that after the offer had been explored in this way the energy created around the offer would be of sufficient 'charge' and detail that it was now unavoidable to those in the scene. They would then begin to work *re-actively* off the offers which surrounded them. This enabled them to take the focus off pushing and straining to make the scene 'happen', and to simply embrace the possibilities as they presented themselves.

Application Using this basic concept, I have adapted its use to the audition speech. This exercise offers the actor an opportunity to plunge into each of the ideas and to physically and emotionally explore exactly what lies behind or indeed beyond the words. As I have mentioned before, it fuses at once intellectual understanding with *sensation* and aims to pinpoint the precise energy fuelling each thought.

Point of concentration To verbally unearth the dominant meaning beyond the words.

ILLUSTRATION 1

Extend/Advance can be done with someone else side-coaching or you can select the moments yourself.

Clear a space so you have some room to move. You may need to have your script open and accessible as once you begin extending you may lose your place in the text.

Take a moment to focus your energies on the scene. Allow yourself to imaginatively connect to the person you are interacting with or, if the character is alone, to the situation or dilemma facing him or her.

When you're ready, say the first line. Then choose *one word* or an *image* in the line that you wish to explore. Say the word, then extend its meaning using your own words and phrases. For example, if the word is 'large', you could extend by saying: 'large... big... enormous... gigantic... powerful... awesome... *overwhelming*'.

Note: Be sure you extend based on *sensation.* In other words, avoid extending in a monotone as if you were reading from a Thesaurus. It's not mental and verbal gymnastics. Let your *sensory impulses* enter the exercise. Only then will you uncover the essence of each thought and connect emotionally.

'Large' can mean all of the definitions listed above and more. But 'overwhelming' may be exactly the thought which lies behind the word. As you extend, this detailing allows you time to live with the thought, to ruminate on its meaning. If the line was, 'This is a very large problem for me', by allowing the thought *'overwhelming'* to affect the word 'large', it changes the choice and specifies what you are trying to make understood with the idea. Now try saying the line aloud with this thought in mind and feel how easy it is to inhabit the line now that the idea behind it has been uncovered. Communication becomes active and you will feel your energy releasing.

Michael Shurtleff states that 'communication is duplication'; you're attempting to duplicate your thoughts and feelings within the other character, to gain the desired reaction or response. Many actors get too locked into their character's overall objective. This objective is *not* the major focus of the scene- the main priority is to change the other person's *will.* You have more chance of achieving this if you cease worrying about making them *feel* what you're feeling and allow them to *understand* your feelings, moment by moment. Only through uncovering the specific idea behind each thought will you achieve accurate and effective communication.

You may find through working with this exercise that your choice of 'overwhelming' makes the character too much of a victim and is not appropriate for that point in the play. Therefore, extend again in another direction, such as 'large... difficult... tricky... elusive... provocative... *challenging!*

Now the choice has shifted. The character has changed his or her attitude toward the situation and the idea behind the thought has altered. We receive different information from the character through his or her exchange. By exploring the possibilities of what may work best for the scene, you clarify each choice and its meaning, and in turn create the *score.*

Of course, working in this detail produces the other essential component of your speech — ownership. Through using *Extend/ Advance* you will *personalise* each thought, *claim* its essential energy, and it will become (if done correctly) *sensation.*

This will then form part of the physical infrastructure of your piece. In your rehearsal you will have inhabited the *physical dynamics* associated with the words. If done in enough detail, these dynamics will be triggered again by the sheer act of *saying* the words in the audition.

The effect is much like when you look back through an old photograph album. Because you have experienced (personalised) all of the sensations associated with each and every photo, you don't have to work to produce sensation. The image triggers all the required sets of responses. You simply allow each stimulus entry, and your reactions take care of themselves. The emotional landscape or backdrop to each 'offer' has already been prepared. The same vivid associations occur with particular songs we hear which plug into a certain experience or time in our lives.

Trust then in your rehearsal preparation and at your audition (much like the photograph album) simply focus on each offer line by line, and react to them as they present themselves.

Note: After using this exercise on text you may find each thought becomes overloaded with meaning. By immersing yourself in that meaning the line may appear overly emphasised. The next stage is to trust the work you have done and allow it to affect your acting in whatever way you feel is most appropriate to the character and the situation.

ILLUSTRATION 2

Using *Extend/Advance*, let's look in detail at Natalia Petrovna's scene from Ivan Turgenev's, *A Month in the Country.* Natalia has, unknowingly, fallen in love with her ward's tutor. Vera, after extensive and provocative questions from Natalia, finally declares *her* love for the young, handsome Beliaev. Upon hearing the child's innocent admission, Natalia suddenly feels faint and distressed and sends Vera from the room. She attempts to deal with her strange and disconcerting emotional dilemma. Let's look at her first four lines:

NATALIA: *These children love each other... Well, it's a touching idea, and may Heaven bless them both. The way she came out with it... and I with no idea* — (laughing feverishly) — *ha!* (Rising, vehement.) *But all is not lost — oh no...'*

We'll now apply *Extend/Advance* to unearth what may be driving each thought:

'*These children love each other...*' Extend '*children*' — children... innocents... vulnerable beings... *young pure lovers*. Advance: '*Well, it's a touching idea...*'. Extend '*touching*' — touching... simple... pleasant... *quaint.* Advance: '... *And may Heaven bless them both*'. Extend '*bless*' — bless... anoint... keep safe... look after... *guard and protect*. Advance: '*The way she came out with it...* '. Extend '*out with it*' — out with it... blurting it forth... freely expressing... captivating in its innocence... *an absolute admission*. Advance: '*and I with no idea*'. Extend '*no idea*' — no idea... not the faintest clue... never suspected... never dreamed of... *couldn't have possibly expected.* Advance: '*ha!*'. Extend '*ha!*' — ha!... quite extraordinary!... I never expected this!... An absolute surprise!... *Quite a substantial shock!!!* Advance: '*But all is not lost, oh no...*'. Extend '*not lost*' — not lost... not forsaken... within my grasp... *still ultimately achievable!*

Through the extensions Natalia's interior world becomes more defined. She's taken aback by Vera's honesty and vulnerability *(young pure lovers),* and her efforts to shield and detach herself from the hurt and her inevitable downfall become clear *(It's a touching idea.)*. You have now begun to process the thoughts, forming personal responses to each idea. Her attitude to her situation has become defined (see Plate 2).

The journey through your extensions can lead you from your *head,* as a place where the thoughts originate, to your *heart*, where you feel certain emotions and sensations, to your *centre* — the pit of your stomach where instinct and 'gut' reactions reside. It's this third level where raw and highly concentrated connections are forged.

To assist actors in remembering these connections, I ask them to repeat the line after the extension. For example, with the extension on the word 'touching', we hit upon the word 'quaint'. Retaining this attitude of slight condescension and jealousy, repeat the entire line, 'Well, it's a *touching* idea...'. This allows the discoveries made during the extension to inform the line when repeated. There's not much point embarking on a tremendously potent exploration of the thought's essence if on your return the line retains its original attachments and quality.

The same applies to the next extension: 'bless'. After uncovering '*guard and protect*', retain her attitude of mock care and seeming unperturbed resignation and repeat the line with both extensions: 'Well, it's a *touching* idea, and may Heaven *bless* them both.'

ILLUSTRATION 3

You may also want to extend *within* an extension. For example, during the last extension on 'not lost', we arrived at '*still ultimately achievable*'. This uncovered Natalia's selfishness and her ability for deceitful manipulation. Allowing this to fuel your journey, extend '*achievable*' — achievable... capable of being embraced... winnable... *I refuse to lose*. Extend '*lose*' — lose... be lost... forgotten... thrown on the heap... discarded... *grow old*. Extend '*grow old*' — grow old... become aged... withered... decrepit and despised... never having *tasted passion*. Extend '*tasted*' — touched... stroked... caressed... *entwined*. Extend '*passion*' — passion... romance... unbridled sensuality... ultimate sacrifice... complete union... *pleasure beyond all limits!!*

Now, allow the depth of this journey to rocket you back to the beginning of the line, keeping all that you have found: '*But all is not lost — oh no...*'. The full scope of Natalia's fear and power begins to emerge.

This work enlivens the unconscious, provoking deep associations and strong energy productions — your speech is charged with your imprint and your acting is informed.

The example from *A Month in the Country* shows *Extend/Advance* working on a soliloquy. It can prove as effective in a slightly different way when dealing with a scene. On these extensions, not only can you explore the *images* but also the *effect* you wish to have on the other character. In other words, if when you're extending you find you begin to challenge, confront, cajole, entreat, then allow the extension to amplify *this*. As such, both your *connection* to the thought *and* the way you *communicate* that thought become more specific.

ILLUSTRATION 4

Take a scene in Arthur Miller's *All My Sons*. George returns to the Keller household to stop his sister, Ann, from marrying the son of Joe Keller, whom George believes is responsible for his father's imprisonment.

> GEORGE: *Annie, we did a terrible thing. We can never be forgiven. Not even to send him a card at Christmas.*

Using these first few lines we'll extend both the image and the effect being created.

> '*Annie, we did a terrible thing.*' Extend '*terrible*' — terrible... cruel... we punished our father wrongly... you and I abused him and caused him great pain... it was *wrong and we were fools.*
>
> The effect on Ann could be one of *admonishment.*

Advance: '*We can never be forgiven*'. Extend '*never*' — never... as long as we live... no matter how hard we try or how much we beg to be unburdened of the guilt... we are *forever tainted.*

> The effect here may be one of *illumination.*

Advance: '*Not even to send him a card at Christmas*'. Extend '*not even*' — not even... we couldn't even muster that... not even an attempt or a gesture... we were so full of self-righteousness... so sure of ourselves.... absolutely *high and mighty* .

> George now *ridicules* himself and Ann in an effort to make her understand the consequences of their actions.

Extend/Advance helps gain specific and detailed connections to the inner life of the character and allows your *score* to be revealed and clarified. Use it whenever you feel a deeper contact and a greater degree of specificity is needed.

EXERCISE 2: Speeches Within Speeches

Choosing Your Beats

Let us now look at beats and how a speech can be divided into certain units of action. Once you have chosen your beats you can then explore and heighten certain aspects of them in order to test their dynamic potential.

Explanation Each beat (sometimes called a unit) revolves around or concerns itself with, an issue — an aspect of the character's situation or dilemma. A beat is a section of the text or a group of thoughts which deal with this specific part of the character's objective.

Much like you acknowledge the punctuation in the speech to help claim the thought process, plotting the beats is like deciphering the scene's *psychological* punctuation. If the structure of each sentence is a direct expression of the character's thought process, the structure of the beats is a direct expression of the character's emotional process.

Robert Benedetti points out that the stylistics of language reflect the personality and characteristics of the speaker, and to enter the character's consciousness you must claim not only what the character says, but *how* he or she says it. This applies also to the psychological journey — claim not only what happens to the character, but also the sequence and consequence of *how* it affects him or her. The beats represent and clarify this journey. The actor can then feel no longer burdened with the weight of attempting to achieve the scene's full depth and power through every moment. But he or she can trust the *journey* which has been securely plotted, and allow the *sum* of all the individual moments and beats to produce the scene's impact.

Once the beats have been uncovered you may want to assign each of them a name or title (see Plate 2). This is *not* done as an intellectual exercise but as a way of plotting the emotional journey through the scene. It will help you to avoid the speech becoming one entire entity embellished with one emotion or set of responses. Lisle Jones always suggests the actor 'find the speeches *within* the speech'.

Application To avoid scenes and indeed speeches from being swamped by a particular dynamic and emotional bias. By plotting the beats, we aim to uncover the *structure* of the speech. This structure becomes a pathway along which we can plot the character's journey. From here, we ensure maximum emotional range and specific detail.

Point of concentration Through our experience of the speech, we aim to locate major shifts in the scene's energy and direction.

ILLUSTRATION 1

Let's look at a scene from *Wild Honey* by Anton Chekhov, translated and adapted by Michael Frayn. Following is one version of the speech divided into *five* beats. It often comes down to your own interpretation and no one way is the correct way.

Anna Petrovna has followed her potential lover Platanov into the garden at night. Both of them, married to other partners (she now widowed), bemoan the fact that their lives have gone in separate directions. Their discussion leads to an unspecified past 'liaison' which Platanov seemingly dismisses as a figment of her imagination. Turning towards him, the forest surrounding them and a midsummer night's breeze touching the air, she responds:

ANNA PETROVNA: *How can you say that? How can you lie to me, on such a night as this, beneath such a sky? Tell your lies in the autumn, if you must, in the gloom and the mud, but not now, not here.* ①

You're being watched! Look up, you absurd man! A thousand eyes, all shining with indignation! You must be good and true, just as all this is good and true. Don't break this silence with your little words! ... ②

There's no man in the world I could ever love as I love you. There's no woman in the world you could ever love as you love me. Let's take that love; and all the rest, that so torments you — we'll leave that to others to worry about. ③

Such a solemn face! It's a woman who's come to call, not a wild animal! All right — if you really hate it all so much I'll go away again. Is that what you want? I'll go away, and everything will be just as it was before. Yes...?

(She laughs.)

Idiot! Take it! Snatch it! Seize it! What more do you want? Smoke it to the end, like a cigarette — pinch it out — tread it under your heel. Be human! ④

(She gently shakes him.)

You funny creature! A woman who loves you — a woman you love — fine summer weather. What could be simpler than that?...

You don't realise how hard life is for me. And yet life is what I long for. Everything is alive nothing is ever still. We're surrounded by life. We must live, too, Misha! Leave all the problems for tomorrow. Tonight, on this night of nights, we'll simply live! ⑤

A fairly convincing argument! As you can see, I have marked *five* beats. Each beat can be viewed as a separate speech within the speech. This will assist us in opening up the scene's range to produce a dynamic emotional journey.

Now, look at each beat in detail — observe the major thrust of that beat. What similar ideas fuel the beat ? Which of the character's needs drives it, and what does the character wish to achieve ? If there was one *key phrase* which summed up that beat or unit, which would it be? For example:

Beat 1: No lies... *'not now, not here'*.
Beat 2: *'Don't break this silence...'*
Beat 3: *'Let's take that love...'*
Beat 4: *'Be human!'*
Beat 5: *'...we'll simply live!'*

These lines distil the character's specific wants, beat by beat. They also clearly show the speech's journey. It is much like an exercise where you concentrate your scene down to a telegram format, which demands you choose the half dozen most important moments without which the speech would not make sense. It enables you to narrow the aperture to focus on the speech's essence, so the major turning points and events become palpable.

Remember: working for form and end results can significantly reduce range and ownership. Many actors have worked this piece with me, *beginning* their rehearsal process by attempting to inhabit Anna Petrovna's feisty nature, her sensuality, passion and independence. Yes, she is all these things, but they are by-products of the *action* of the scene — what *happens*. *This* must be our starting point.

Therefore the journey for Anna Petrovna begins with Beat 1 — her refusal to accept Platanov's way of looking at their relationship *(*don't lie... *'not now, not here')*. In Beat 2 she requests he doesn't say anything to contaminate the intimacy possible between them *('Don't break this silence with your little words')*. In Beat 3 she proposes she and Platanov, against all the odds, rejuvenate their passion and commitment *('Let's take that love...')*. In Beat 4, because of Platanov's hopeless outlook he resists his feelings and instincts, provoking her to exclaim: *'Be human!'*. He now begins to be affected by her vulnerability, and so in Beat 5 she expounds one final thought, made of reckless passion and graceful ease: *'Tonight, on this night of nights, we'll simply live!'*

Actors so often view the speech as a total entity and find one or two dynamics or qualities which, as mentioned earlier, can swamp the entire text. Each of the five sections can now be explored for their *unique* and *essential* energy, enabling you to extend the character's and the scene's range. EXERCISE 3 will begin this work but let's first look more closely at Beats.

Beat Changes

Explanation The next thing to explore is what initiates one beat to end and another to begin. Something must *happen* for the scene to change direction. These moments are called *beat changes*, and denote an *event*. Beat changes occur when a character changes objective, or alters his or her tactics sufficiently to create a new energy in the scene, *or* achieves his or her desired result and a new objective begins. Sometimes they can be spotted clearly on the page but other times they will emerge only through the playing of the scene and through your *experiencing* of the action.

Application When you have plotted the beat changes it means by necessity you have observed the events through the speech. Plays are written about events: crises, disclosures, deceits, tragedies, triumphs, reconciliations — occurrences which speak of the human condition.

> Playwrights register and record the tremors of this world.[16]

These 'tremors' manifest themselves in the events which the characters experience. Once acknowledged through your acting, they begin to release the play's action. The nature and impact of these events will then chart an emotional journey which, to our best knowledge, will articulate the playwright's intentions.

How you plot beat changes and the events which produce them again depends upon your interpretation.

Point of concentration To reveal the *events* which promote the major shifts in the scene's energy and direction.

ILLUSTRATION 1

Beat 1 of Anna Petrovna's scene culminates in her successfully prohibiting Platanov from dismissing their passionate past, for he says no more.

Because of that event, she then, in Beat 2, enlists the forces of nature, which charge the atmosphere surrounding them with a pure energy. Her actions cause an intimacy between them to be rekindled, which Platanov struggles to avoid. At the end of this Beat she touches her finger to his lips in an attempt to retain the purity and potency of their moment. This she achieves.

Because of *this* event, in Beat 3 she can now speak with extreme candour. She consequently offers him an escape back to what they once shared, but she sees this only depresses him, as he views her suggestion as fruitless and impossible.

Because of *this* event, she states in Beat 4 that she will leave him forever, forlorn and lost. She therefore proposes that he take all that life has to offer. She concludes they both love each other and nothing could be simpler. This event affects him in that she is reaching him and he can perhaps resist no longer.

In the final and most important Beat, Anna Petrovna now reveals her fragility and vulnerability. She concludes that this special moment is for them, that they must live, and that their relationship must be reborn so as to save them. The main event of the scene is that he agrees, and as the fireworks explode across the night sky, they exit into the shadows of the forest.

Each beat culminates in an *event* — something *happens* which alters the energy and direction of the scene. A journey becomes clear as we have revealed the structure behind the lines and can now release each beat's fullest potential. In essence, we have deciphered the overall score of the scene.

Notice that I haven't used words which emotionally charge the choices: Anna Petrovna *exclaims*, she *suggests*, she *offers*, she *clarifies*, she *expounds*, she *invokes*, she *concludes*. I haven't entered into *how* she goes about doing these things. That's for you to discover through your rehearsal. How *provocative*, *dismissive*, *challenging, seductive* she is depends upon your interpretation.

ILLUSTRATION 2

Following are three more examples of speeches divided into their beats.

Firstly, read Bubba's speech from Ray Lawler's *Summer of the Seventeenth Doll.* She talks to Roo and Barney after the drama and conflict of the preceding night. Dowdie has asked her out and she tells the two men for the first time of her true feelings and needs.

BUBBA: *It's no use tryin' to talk me out of it, Roo... He sent you out of the room and told me not to... to take any notice of what you said.* ①

Then he asked me... He asked me! And he didn't call me B-Bubba or kid, he wanted to know what my real name was, and when I told him, that's what he called me. Kathie. ②

[She turns away to ROO.]

He might have been drinking, and this morning he might have forgotten like you said, but this is the only chance I've ever had of comin' close to — I dunno — whatever it is I've been watching all these years. You think I'll give that up?... ③

Dolls and breaking things, and — and arguments about who was best — what do they all matter? That wasn't the lay-off... ④

I'll have what you had — the real part of it — but I'll have it differently. Some way I can have it safe and know that it's going to last... ⑤

No matter what happens, I'll always remember you, 'n' this house, 'n' the lay-off. ⑥

Now that you've read the scene and seen the six beats as I have marked them, choose each beat's *key phrase* — the phrase without which the beat would lose its focus, drive and meaning. This will give you a strong insight into the plot or action of the beat and of course, its function. Do this exercise for yourself before reading on.

Here are the key lines as I interpret them: Beat 1 - *No use*; Beat 2 - *He asked me!*; Beat 3 - *the only chance*; Beat 4 - *What do they matter?*; Beat 5 - *That's going to last*; Beat 6 - *I'll always remember you.*

If you have chosen effectively, the six key phrases when read together should tell the story of the speech by themselves — they should distil the essential meaning and chart the speeches journey. Each key phrase should also relate to every line *within* the beat — in other words, your chosen key phrase represents the main idea driving that beat, and all other lines surrounding it shape that idea.

Look at the following speech from *Henry VI – Part One*. Joan la Pucelle visits Charles with a very clear objective in mind. The speech has four beats — each one becomes a building block in which Joan attempts to change the Dauphin's will by leading him towards her vision of how things could be.

JOAN:
Dolphin, I am by birth a shepherd's daughter,
My wit untrained in any kind of art.
Heaven and our Lady gracious hath it please ①
To shine on my contemptible estate.

Lo, whilst I waited on my tender lambs,
And to sun's parching heat displayed my cheeks,
God's mother deigned to appear to me,
And in a vision, full of majesty, ②
Willed me to leave my base vocation
And free my country from calamity.
Her aid she promised, and assured success.

In complete glory she revealed herself—
And whereas I was black and swart before,
With those clear rays which she infused on me ③
That beauty am I blest with, which you may see.

Ask me what question thou canst possible,
And I will answer unpremeditated.
My courage try by combat, if thou dar'st,
And thou shalt find that I exceed my sex. ④
Resolve on this: thou shalt be fortunate,
If thou receive me for they warlike mate.

This time I have given each beat a title — it works in a similar way to the key phrase — the title sums up the main idea which fuels the beat. It also serves as a reminder as to exactly what the other person must *understand* if you are indeed to change their mind and therefore achieve your objective.

Beat 1; *I have been chosen*. Beat 2; *I had a vision of freedom - victory*. Beat 3; *I am transformed*. Beat 4; *Our crusade begins!*

An excellent rehearsal technique is to repeat the title of the beat after each line of the text (using major punctuation as your guide, *ie* a full-stop, exclamation mark, colon, semi-colon and question mark). You will find this a very effective way in which to charge each line with an energy and focus its impact. It will invest meaning and give you an aim to everything you say and do onstage, *ie*:

Dolphin, I am by birth a shepherd's daughter,
My wit untrained in any kind of art.
Yet I have been chosen!
Heaven and our Lady gracious hath it pleased
To shine on my contemptible estate.
I have been chosen!!

Choose whatever title propels you into action. Use any words which catapult you away from 'inventing' in order to be correct, towards an organic connection to the reality of who you are and what you are there to do.

Lastly, look at Rosalind's speech from *As You Like It.* Once again, four very clear beats. Once you are clear on the sense of the speech — which will mean a line by line literal translation — look at the beat titles. Use the title after each line of the text and observe how they empower the words, shaping ideas and making every moment of the scene a movement into the future. (Remember: use major punctuation).

ROSALIND:
And why, I pray you? Who might be your mother,
'That you insult, exult, and all at once,
Over the wretched? What though you have no beauty —
As, by my faith, I see no more in you ①
Than without candle may go dark to bed —
Must you be therefore proud and pitiless?

Why, what means this? Why do you look on me?
I see no more in you than in the ordinary
Of nature's sale-work. — Odd's my little life,
I think she means to tangle my eyes, too!
No, faith, proud mistress, hope not after it. ②
'Tis not your inky brows, your black silk hair,
Your bugle eyeballs, nor you cheek of cream,
That can entame my spirits to your worship.

[To SILVIUS] *You, foolish shepherd, wherefore do you follow her*
Like foggy south, puffing with wind and rain?
You are a thousand times a properer man
Than she a woman. 'Tis such fools as you

That makes the world full of ill-favoured children.
'Tis not her glass but you that flatters her, ③
And out of you she sees herself more proper
Than any of her lineaments can show her.

[To PHEBE] *But, mistress, know yourself; down on your knees*
And thank heaven, fasting, for a good man's love;
For I must tell you friendly in you ear,
Sell when you can. You are not for all markets.
Cry the man mercy, love him, take his offer; ④
Foul is most foul, being foul to be a scoffer. —
So, take her to thee, shepherd. Fare you well.

Beat 1; You are so full of pride and arrogance! Beat 2; I can't give you anything you desire! Beat 3; Don't be a fool for love! Beat 4; Wake up and smell the coffee!!!

Now we want to *further* seek out what is possible. The preparation has been done, the launching pad is secure; our exploration continues.

EXERCISE 3: Explore and Heighten

This exercise derives from a Viola Spolin exercise. Once again I have adapted the concept to text. It was developed as a tool to help release particular emotional dynamics from an improvisation.

Explanation After the improvisation, the teacher suggests the scene be re-enacted but this time the actors are asked to develop, as often as possible, *one aspect* of the scene. For example, if the scenario is a first date, then whenever possible, *explore* through the scene, then *heighten* whenever possible, the embarrassment, the sexual attraction, the need to impress, or indeed the silences. Once heightened, each element brings a different dimension to the scene. Through this exploratory work you will find aspects which release the scene's dramatic essence.

Application This exercise can be used as effectively with text. You might find the dynamics arising from your exploration suddenly suit the words and the interaction. As a result, you may have moved one step closer to revealing the playwright's intentions. As opposed to Extend/Advance, which deals with specific word/idea meaning, this exercise focuses on the particular *issues* which certain beats reveal. It also offers us the chance to probe particular dimensions of the character's emotional condition.

Point of concentration To allow the chosen dimension being explored to impact upon the beat, and for this aspect to be released through the scene's action.

ILLUSTRATION 1

You can choose to explore and heighten any element you feel will help release the scene's life and extend its range. With the previous scene from *Wild Honey*, you could embrace and amplify any of the following: Anna Petrovna's recklessness, passion, intimacy, seductiveness, innocence, manipulation, loneliness, desperation, sexual prowess.

With your beats chosen, elect *one* beat and explore a particular, and perhaps appropriate, dimension. After looking at the dimension of the character I have chosen to heighten below, keep it clear in your mind while you re-read the corresponding beat and observe any changes which occur.

Beat 1: Amplify her defiance. (Now read Beat 1.)
Beat 2: Amplify her magnetism.
Beat 3: Amplify her sensual potency.
Beat 4: Amplify her appetite for the reckless.
Beat 5: Amplify her hunger for all life has to offer.

This exploration should reveal what drives the beat. But it may also prove ineffective and therefore point your search in another direction. Or you may find it releases exactly the right energy for the scene on only a *few* of the lines. This is precisely what the rehearsal period is for — provoking what's possible, pushing the boundaries of the character's expression, plunging into the depths of the scene's dynamic range.

> Theatre is the result of a collision of values. Through this collision we gain insight and understanding. [17]

Use *Explore and Heighten* to pinpoint, then provoke each of the character's values or issues which collide head-on in each beat. For example: Beat 1 — her truth *vs* his fabrication; Beat 2 — her intimacy *vs* his sense of responsibility; Beat 3 — her passion *vs* his fear; Beat 4 — her freedom *vs* his restraint; Beat 5 — her surrender *vs* his temptation which leads to acceptance.

Because acting is the passionate pursuit of an objective, obstacles can therefore produce great passion.

The issues above highlight the many obstacles Anna Petrovna has to deal with. These issues provide potent stimuli within the speech which you can react off. They provoke *actions* which lead to developing the score of the speech.

Remember to allow the dimension you are heightening to be revealed through this interaction and not merely tacked on as an emotional state or characteristic. It doesn't mean Anna's character is *powerful* throughout the beat, but there will be moments when her strength of will and purpose will become active and dominant and she is able to affect powerful change in Platanov. The chosen aspect *translates* into action. Once again, don't play the effect: connect to its cause.

ILLUSTRATION 2

Some frequently performed speeches, like Hamlet's *'O, what a rogue and peasant slave am I!'*, are often done with one characteristic dominating the scene. As such, the entire text swims in an emotional wash of either seething anger, uncontrolled rage, mild philosophical musing or a maudlin and inactive depression. The actor begins by taking a deep breath then proceeds to, very successfully, explore and heighten *one aspect* of the character's world. This limits the scene's range and inhibits the dynamics possible. But through uncovering the beats in the scene, you may find the above mentioned aspects *all* appear in some form at some stage.

Hamlet has moments where he abases himself and despises his inactivity. He then tries to comprehend his predicament. From here he attempts to take the path of direct, positive action. But more the fool he, for he discovers that this path alludes him. As a result of his inability to act, the pressures become a battle where he hits out at the world at large for thinking him a coward. He then acknowledges his lack of courage and inner weakness. Through his emotional miasma he makes the dilemma surrounding him concrete and elucidates what exactly should be done. He rails to the gods and calls forth his only ally and saviour, *'O, vengeance!'*

Discover firstly the beats, then uncover what is peculiar to each beat. In other words, what function does it serve? To help find this out, ask what the speech would lose if the beat were to be cut? You'll soon see what purpose it serves and that will give you powerful clues as to what your rehearsal needs to focus on.

ILLUSTRATION 3
In later rehearsals you may want to explore and heighten aspects of the scene other than those already mentioned. For example:

- the pre-life to the scene — what has just affected the character.
- the discoveries the character makes (see EXERCISE 6).
- the inner tension or preoccupation the character may be experiencing.
- the conditions which surround the character, such as the temperature and other climactic elements.
- the setting — forest, beach, boardroom. Each environment can have is own effect on the scene.
- the knowledge that someone may overhear or indeed enter.
- the conflict.
- the dilemma.
- the potency of the inner monologue (see EXERCISE 4).
- the impact of the events.

All of these dimensions can contribute to your onstage reality and create atmosphere. They offer various dynamics which can inform your acting and help release the scene's depth and quality. You can now choose what works and plot it in as part of the scene's journey.

Allow *Explore and Heighten* to stimulate your imagination and provide an arena for your creative exploration of the issues driving each beat. The result will be a strong and vivid belief in all you do and your speech will show an extensive range of the character's emotional life.

EXERCISE 4: Inner Monologue/Departures

Application If we could record on a disk someone's inner thoughts — his or her most intimate reactions, second by second, to all he or she encountered, and if this disc was to be lodged in *our* nerve centre, we would know what it is to *be* someone else. To embrace another's inner perception in this deeply subjective way would lead us to the inner core of his or her being and reveal the person's psyche. As a result, we would experience the *sensations* from which spring all the person says and does.

This is also the realm from which a *character's* reality is formed. Obviously then, it will be advantageous to us as actors to inhabit a character's inner thoughts — in essence, to *think* as the character would, not as the actor.

It is always interesting to observe the actor's degree of such internal focus on an opening night. No matter how skilled the 'performance' of the role, letters passed onstage shake, brims of hats quiver, any intricate action requires extra concentration. Hence the lighting of a cigarette, an ordinary daily activity performed with little thought, suddenly demands dexterity and a high level of skill. On that all too important opening the actor's inner monologue affects the character's world.

But return to the production perhaps only a few performances later and a *fusion* has taken place: an actor/character melding of the internal and the external worlds. The character's deep inner thoughts and perceptions have been embraced by the *actor's* inner workings. All intricate action now appears totally natural, unconscious. The actor now seems to own and inhabit his or her onstage world with complete surety.

In an audition you do not have the luxury of a performance season to find this fusion. Therefore, your rehearsal period must at some point focus on the character's deep inner workings so that, under pressure, you can still feel released and at ease within your character's reality.

Explanation This exercise contributes to the fusion referred to above. You can use it alone or someone else can be your side-coach. As before, have your script handy. Most of these rehearsal room exercises shake up what we know and enable us to discard old patterns. Trying to remember lines and what comes next are the last things you want to expend energy on.

Once again, concentrate your internal energies on the situation. Begin when you feel connected to your first need.

If you have someone working with you, he or she should direct you at some point during the speech to release *out loud* the character's inner thoughts *at that instant*. On the instruction 'Inner monologue', simply plug into that internal disc mentioned earlier and allow the character's deep subjectivity in that moment to fuel your departure. Experience the myriad of thoughts and sensations rocketing through the character's nervous system. It doesn't matter what you say — it's not poetry, nor does it even have to make sense. It is for no one's benefit but your own.

After somewhere between six and a dozen of your own lines, your side-coach should direct you to 'Play on'. At this point, return to the script and allow your next line to be *affected* by your inner monologue departure. Remember: The energy in the scene should now be *different*. Allow an inner journey to take place which will charge the scene ahead.

Point of concentration To plug into and experience the character's deep subjective thinking process and to allow its vivid and muscular quality to affect the ensuing moment.

ILLUSTRATION 1

During Nina's speech to her psychiatrist in Anthony Minghella's screenplay, *Truly, Madly, Deeply*, she speaks about Jamie, her deceased fiance:

First read the dialogue in italics *only,* then include the inner monologue departure examples allowing them to affect your *re-reading* of the scene.

NINA

Mostly when I'm walking, at night, or anyway, alone, if I'm frightened, then he'll turn up...

Inner monologue: 'out of nowhere, suddenly *beamed-in* beside me... with that extraordinary familiarity... that feeling... affirming... he *knew* me completely. We had *recognition*. (Play on.)

...he'll, he'll talk, about what I'm doing...

Inner monologue: 'because you see I was scared, and always a bit of a klutz and he... he'd instruct me, that's how it felt, and it helped... he cared.' (Play on.)

...you know, some advice, he'll say — 'Don't be frightened. I've told you — walk in the middle of the road at night.

Inner monologue: 'He'd sort of lose patience with me, but he was joking. He had such kind eyes. Love does that.' (Play on.)

And I will, I move over to the middle of the road, or, I don't know, he'll say: 'It's a disgrace, this street is a disgrace, there's no proper lighting, have you written, you must write!'

Inner monologue: 'I'd love it when he became militant and wanted to change the world. He'd get all feisty and fired up. He pushed me from my safe-zone... challenged me. (Play on.)

He's always forthright, I mean he always was forthright so I suppose that's not, but, you know...

Inner monologue: 'Christ, the blackness — the wasteland — get it together! You can't go on, you haven't got the energy — search, speak more, find a new distraction...' (Play on.)

... he'll also speak in Spanish to me, which is odd because he couldn't speak Spanish —

Inner monologue: 'it's pointless remembering all this, it's like hot pokers slicing through my stomach, but... you must... deal with... how can I move on... I... don't lose it... keep going... face it...' (Play on.)

and I would be feeling low, you know, very alone and hopeless and — and then he's there, his presence, and it's okay, it's fine, and I don't mind and he tells me he loves me.

Inner monologue: 'I remember his lips — his eyelashes — when he spoke of love the air changed. The incredible *ease* I felt — unburdened and protected. I breathed fresh breath and seemed to *know* more.. He *became* my longing'. (Play on.)

And then he's not there any more.

Inner monologue: 'But it lasts — his touch. It stays within and sleeps with me for days. Stupid, I know. He knows just when the blackness... the void... descends... opens... he... just... knows, and...' (Play on.)

...I feel looked after, I suppose, watched over.

(Now re-read the dialogue *and* the inner monologue departures.)

Nina's *interior* world becomes a part of the scene's tapestry. Her public interaction and her private thoughts and feelings begin to work in tandem and the associations made on the departures empower the text. This works in a similar way to *Extend/Advance* but offers a greater scope for the broader, general thoughts surrounding the text. The departures can also develop strong atmospheric dynamics within the scene. The example above is only *one* interpretation. Each actor will embody the scene differently. It is this aspect of the inner monologue which will mark the speech as distinctly your own.

Note that there are two options you can take on your return:

1. Release the inner feelings you stirred during the departure.
2. Hide them and keep them as private thoughts.

Either way (and it may change from line to line as the speech progresses), allow the scene to *develop* and be *altered* in response to the specific inner dynamic with which you return.

ILLUSTRATION 2

For example, if in a scene you are not getting through to someone you might, on your departure, rant and rave and indulge in every obscenity you can conjure. Then, after the 'play on', you may smile and look completely rational and together, with not a care in the world — happy and content to once more state your case and work towards a resolution. But, as a result of your departure, as you begin to speak your *over*-politeness and *accentuated* genuineness tells the audience that something's got to give. Comedy in a scene is often heightened significantly when the pressure of the inner monologue is so great it requires containment. Even though you may choose to conceal your inner thoughts in this way, your departure has changed the energy and dynamic tension of the scene and therefore moved the scene forward.

The *Inner Monologue Departures* stir the sub-text — the thoughts behind the lines. They also assist you in discovering the life-blood of the character and creating an inner foundation from which the character's outer world can spring.

EXERCISE 5: 'Is This Good or Bad for Me?' [18]

Sometimes at an audition the comments from the panel focus on a similar theme: 'the actor didn't appear connected'; 'didn't work off the other actor'; 'skimmed across the surface'; 'it all seemed too performed and predictable'; 'it didn't engage me'.

One major factor often evident in auditions is the actor's inability to *process* the scene. Processing entails three stages:

1. Acknowledgment of the incoming stimulus, i.e. the other person's reaction, or an idea or thought you have just had.
2. Embracing that stimulus by attaching your attitude to it.
3. Amplifying the stimulus by choosing to react in a particular way which will affect change in the other person, or within yourself (if for example, doing a soliloquy).

The lack of processing can be a danger for actors during long runs. In such cases, the choices made, moment by moment, often become not choices but *decisions*, and are not provoked by incoming stimulus, but by a pre-learnt and rigid sequence of cues. Here, the actor has inadvertently disengaged from the very process of *choosing* what to do and how to react and is on 'automatic pilot'. The very word 'choice' implies *options.* This process may take only a split second but these options must be entertained before a decision can be reached. By committing to the three stages outlined above, it will lead the actor to being *in the moment* — often referred to as the 'here and now'.

In life we process automatically and every split second. Every stimulus that we register through our senses demands a response from us: a phone ringing, a knock at the door, everything said to us, the tone in a person's voice, the look in his or her eyes. Our response depends on whether what we smell, taste, touch, see or hear is ultimately going to be either good or bad for us. Once our attitude to the stimulus is formed, we have a basis from which to react. We make *conscious* choices. There are also many moments in our day when we react *unconsciously,* purely from instinct, but in this exercise we are concerned with the *conscious* decisions we make when there are options present.

Application The following exercise deals with this aspect of processing. It reminds you to stay in each and every moment and to continue the scene *only* after you have found a *reason* to go on.

I remember the director, Gale Edwards, working with a young actor in an audition. His nerves and desire to *get it right* led him to push through the scene and have little contact with the other character. His eyes seemed glazed as he *worked* the scene and tried to create the effect he was after.

Gale suggested he try the scene again but *this* time to find a reason *within the other character* before he continued on to his next line, i.e. to use the other character's *resistance, annoyance*, *confusion*, or *delight*.

It is the other character's reactions which can become your stimulus — your reason to go on. If you're not getting your desired result or reaction, try another way. If you *are* getting what you want, want *more.* In other words, rather than self-motivating, allow the other character's energy and reactions to be your fuel.

Gale's re-direction took a number of seconds for the actor to process. Up until this point he had been only aware of himself in action. In other words, his focus had been on the inner manufacturing of his emotions and then the external monitoring of their success.

The actor then went to re-enter the scene as he had done, but even here Gale asked him to begin the speech sitting opposite the other actor. In effect, she was releasing him from his set moves that were contributing to him following his pre-learnt sequence of cues.

She reminded him once again to find a reason *within the other actor* to fuel each line. Once understood, and almost immediately as he began, it was as if his sight had been restored — he made contact and dealt with the other actor's energy. He began crafting each idea in an effort to affect change. If the other actor turned away or actually *walked away,* this became a major event. We were now watching an exchange. Even though it was a monologue, it appeared to be a scene (as indeed *all* monologues are). The actor's processing engaged us step by step, moment by moment. His choices *became* choices, and not merely a rehearsed set of decisions.

The following exercise promotes this clear processing and places you firmly in the *here and now*.

Point of concentration To name the exact stimulus affecting you in the moment, and to then attach a *significant* emotional attitude towards that stimulus.

Explanation This can be done on your own or with another actor. After focusing on the scene and your initial need, say your first line. Then deal with whatever you *see* or *imagine* the other character to be doing or thinking and then, in your own words, process its meaning and relevance in terms of your immediate needs.

ILLUSTRATION 1

Let's take a simple first date scenario. You've had dinner, seen the movie, and are presently being dropped off outside your home. The car idles, your leather jacket seems to squeak uncontrollably as you try to decide, 'What next?':

First, read only the speech in italics, then re-read and include the inner processing.

MAN: *What a cold night. I think winter's really on its way now.*

Is this good or bad for me? This is bad, she's looking bored. She's definitely lost interest. Her body seems sort of slumped. I've blown it.

I really enjoyed the movie. The ending was a real shock. I wasn't expecting it.

Is this good or bad for me? This is not just bad, it's pointless. She obviously hated the movie and predicted the ending within two minutes of the start. Her eyes have sort of glazed over now and her fingers are fidgeting like she's loosing patience. This is really bad for me.

Look, I'd better go — I've got some work to catch up on tonight. Thanks again.

Is this good or bad for me? I think it's good — I might be wrong — but she seems slightly disappointed. Her head has turned towards me and she has a slight look of expectation. This could be very good.

I'm up early tomorrow, you know, pretty busy... but... do you, maybe, want to come in for a coffee?

Is this good or bad for me? You bloody idiot! She seems unsure now and hesitant. She's checking her watch. Why did you have to leap into it? Relax. This is getting worse.

It's probably too late. And anyway, (yawning and checking his watch) *is that the time?* (She suddenly turns off the engine.)

Is this good or bad for me? This is becoming highly interesting for me! She looks like she wants to say something. Her head has leaned slightly to the side, her eyes have an expectant quality. Her lips have parted and just now have broken into a slight smile. This could be extraordinarily good!

The 'Is this good or bad for me?' question anchors you to the precise moment. You acknowledge the signals around you, assimilate their meaning, and then attach your attitude. You move into the next moment knowing *what* has just occurred, and *how* you feel towards it. What you choose to *do* because of it depends on the choices you feel are appropriate for the character and the scene.

Actors can become isolated in rehearsals if they place too much emphasis on trying to decide what choice would work best. It can lead them to a clinical search for the end result: 'What should my next moment be? What should the character do?'

I feel it's more beneficial to place your focus on the stimuli you *receive* from the other actor. Claim how *it* makes you feel, then allow yourself to *react.* The old adage that acting is reacting can at times sound too simple, but it offers invaluable advice. Give yourself the permission to *react*, based on your internal processing. Know how something makes you feel then let this sensation lead you to *action*. Discover the acting through the *re*acting.

ILLUSTRATION 2

Let's apply this exercise to a speech. In Louis Nowra's *Sunrise*, Irene talks about her fourteen-year-old daughter, Venice, and her relationship to her father. Irene sees her parents and extended family as disparate and estranged. They have all gathered for a reunion on their father's estate in the South Australian hills.

As before, read only Irene's *dialogue*. After you are familiar with the text, re-read *both* the dialogue *and* the character's inner processing.

IRENE: *She loves him very much.*

Is this good or bad for me? This is bad. Venice sees only the charming things in him, and offers herself to him in a way she never can with me. It's bitterly disappointing — to be loved less. (This is her inner stimulus which will now amplify into her next thought.)

One day I hope she'll go back to Africa and see him as he really is, a marvellous scholar who's gone troppo...

Is this good or bad for me? This memory is very painful. It cuts open my heart and tries to suffocate me. I have no marriage, I feel abandoned and blame myself. It's desolate.

He became so immersed in the language and culture of the people he studied that he became one of them. He used to take Venice to fetish markets — God they're disgusting; putrid smells, monkey heads, dog's teeth, gecko skins...

Is this good or bad for me? This is disturbing. The markets became an obsession. They fuelled his descent into madness. They drew him from me and left me isolated. This memory is painful.

He loved buying them. As souvenirs, he said; but he believed in their powers — Once, when I was in Paris, he took Venice to a tribe who wanted her to help break the drought, because she was white-skinned and blonde like their spirit ancestors...

Is this good or bad for me? This is very confronting. This was the moment I felt I was robbed of my daughter. She was taken from me, and I've been denied access ever since. It disempowered me forever. She was so frightened, so vulnerable. And I could do nothing.

Venice was covered in black grease. Geckos and a goat were slaughtered and their blood poured over her — All the while Alex took pictures. You can see Venice's eyes in the photographs — such terror, such incomprehension! I'll never forgive him for that. She was only seven.

Is this good or bad for me? It is frightening. This was the moment I saw the 'shift' in her life. She would never be the same. I became furious, outraged — yet impotent...

And she still loves him. More than she loves me. Venice has no barriers between her and life. She's like a sponge that soaks up everything.

Is this good or bad for me? This is absolutely unnerving. She has no life-discrimination. She 'absorbs' the world and all its strangeness, daily withdrawing further. It's deeply distressing...

She's in a world I'm not allowed entry into. Even when she was born she had distant eyes. (Smiling) *But what can you expect coming from this background...*

Is this good or bad for me? This is ironic. Here I am again — back home — feeling like the incompetent child, being contaminated by all that surrounds me, undermined at every turn. It's depleting, maddening...

I don't know what I'm going to do with her, David. Sometimes I think she's a normal fourteen-year-old and then... other times I know she's touched.

Is this good or bad for me? It's terrifying. I stand by watching without any ability to affect change. I observe her 'disappearance' minute by minute and blame myself. But I blame more this mess around us and these people who taught us to hate ourselves.

This exercise shows *Irene's memories* to be her stimulus. These associations and all they trigger drive the speech. We see clearly the springboards from one thought to the next and the inner impulses which, once personalised, will allow the actor to *react.* Once this interior work has been specified the *scene* will begin to supply the emotional energy, not the actor. This is the ideal situation for any actor: to be surrounded by circumstances powerful enough to propel you into action, by motivating all you do and say.

The other situation where the exercise is of benefit is in the case of a speech where the dialogue springs from the character's *interaction* with another, such as in the scene from *Wild Honey* where Platanov's reactions, and the events which result, fuel all Anna Petrovna says. If each moment of the scene is not acknowledged, embraced then amplified, you'll end up acting in a void — inventing rather than responding.

ILLUSTRATION 3
Let's look at another play by Louis Nowra. *The Golden Age* tells the story of two young men who come across a lost tribe in the Tasmanian hills. In this scene, Francis follows one of the tribe members, Betsheb, to the river. She fascinates him, and his attraction to her leads him to make further contact.

Remember one of the essential principles in rehearsal is if you're not getting what you want moment by moment, try another way to get it. If you *are* getting what you want, *want* more. Observe this process in the following scene.

Once again, read *only* the dialogue and stage directions first.

[The river, twilight. Betsheb sits, staring out at the evening sun. Francis enters and watches her for some time.]

Is this good or bad for me? This is perfect. She's by herself. She seems calm and relaxed. Her eyes are haunted yet knowing. I must understand her. She holds secrets.

FRANCIS: *Are you looking at the sunset?* [Startled, Betsheb turns around.]

Is this good or bad for me? This is bad. She seems frightened. Her body has become alert. A fear burns in her eyes. She seems poised and prepared to run away. Mustn't lose this opportunity.

[Smiling] *I'm not a monster... No more running.*

Is this good or bad for me? This shows promise. She hasn't run. She's wary though, her hands still grip her thighs, but she seems prepared to test me out. I think this is good.

[Silence. He walks closer to the river.] *Look at us reflected in the water, see? Upside down.*

Is this good or bad for me? This is very good. She's allowed me to get much closer. She's less tense. She's looking in the water. Her face shows fascination by the image. She has become like a child. Relax her more. Calm her. Befriend her.

[He smiles and she smiles back. Silence.]

Is this good or bad for me? This is the most positive sign yet. She's letting me in. She's as curious of me as I am of her.

So quiet. I'm not used to such silence. I'm a city boy, born and bred.

Is this good or bad for me? This is quite strange. Her nostrils flare as if she's trying to smell my very thoughts. She wants to know more.

You've never seen a city or a town, have you? Where I live there are dozens of factories: shoe factories, some that make gaskets, hydraulic machines, clothing. My mother works in a shoe factory. [Pointing to his boots] *These came from my mother's factory.* [Silence.]

Is this good or bad for me? This is extraordinary. She seems transfixed. Unlike any creature I've ever encountered. Her body is supple and receives instinctive impulses. She disarms me — fascinates me. This world I've entered is provoking, haunting...

These sunsets here, I've never seen the likes of them. A bit of muddy orange light in the distance, behind the chimneys, is generally all I get to see.

Is this good or bad for me? This is very good. She smiled again. Her eyes have softened. She's more interested. Her hands play in the dirt and her head leans to the side. She likes me. She wants more.

You'd like the trams, especially at night. They rattle and squeak, like ghosts rattling their chains, and every so often the conducting rod hits a terminus and there is a brilliant spark of electricity, like an axe striking a rock. 'Spiss!'

Is this good or bad for me? This is great. She is completely alive. Her body responds to everything and she's locked in on my energy.

On Saturday afternoon thousands of people go and watch the football. A huge oval of grass. [Miming a football] *A ball like this. Someone hand passes it, 'whish', straight to me. I duck one lumbering giant, spin around a nifty dwarf of a rover, then I catch sight of the goals.*

Is this good or bad for me? This is fantastic. She is totally absorbed. She feeds off all I do and say.

I boot a seventy-yard drop kick straight through the centre. The crowd goes wild! [He cheers wildly. Betsheb laughs at his actions. He is pleased to have made her laugh.]

As you see, the actor's inner processing becomes clear: you acknowledge the stimulus, assimilate its meaning, and then allow your *reaction* to propel the scene forward. This detailed work leads you to inhabit fully the character's moment-by-moment onstage reality. It is this detail which leads the audience through the scene's journey and allows them access to the stage experience.

As a very revealing exercise, watch an international interview on television. Due to the split-second delay as the signals bounce around in outer space, you are privy to a moment normally missed. Because we process so quickly, when viewing a *local* interview we are caught up with our own processing of the question and miss the initial impact on the interviewee. But because of the time delay in an international interview, that precious split second is revealed — we have already ascertained whether *we* regard the question's impact as good or bad, so are afforded the luxury of witnessing that precise moment when the person on the receiving end does the same. The more tricky or confronting the question the more accentuated this moment will become.

Use 'Is this good or bad for me?' whenever you wish to clarify the moment-by-moment interaction. It reveals inner motivation and amplifies the choice-making process, engaging the audience on a fundamental and essential level.

EXERCISE 6: Major Discovery

Application As we have mentioned in the previous exercise, in life we continually deal with our ever-changing environment second by second. Every stimulus received is either hostile or friendly. When translated to the stage, these spontaneous discoveries becomes highly engaging for an audience for they parallel our daily life experience. Watching people 'change', being affected and having to deal with continually mutating sensory information, fascinates us. Life consists of this. Our stage life concentrates and distils this process, providing life-parallels and therefore, a mirror to nature — the essence of the theatre experience.

Great plays are written around great conditions.[19]

You must fully activate your character's sense of *discovery* in order to highlight these great conditions and their effect on you. This will lead to a spontaneous stage life where your awareness of your acting is dissolved and you surrender to the offers around you, and once again, *react.*

Point of concentration To acknowledge every discovery possible in the speech, and to then transform that discovery into *physical* action.

Explanation You will need some room around you in which to move — the larger the space the better.

Allow each discovery the character makes to motivate a physical move somewhere in the space — a run, a turn, a swift walk in a particular direction. In other words, release the emotional revelation through a *physical* impulse.

ILLUSTRATION 1

In Shakespeare's play *All's Well That Ends Well*, Helena has fallen in love with the Countess' son, Bertram. He then departs for the wars without any knowledge of Helena's feelings towards him. After he has gone, Lafew, a courtier, and the Countess see Helena in distress and attribute this to the recent death of her father. They suggest she try to overcome her mourning. They then exit, leaving her alone.

First, simply read the *dialogue,* which is in italics. Then read both the dialogue *and* the discoveries.

LAFEW: *Farewell, pretty lady: you must hold the credit of your father.* [He and the Countess exit.]

HELENA:

Discovery: They think I mourn for my father — crazy — no one knows my secret pain!! (Commit to a physical impulse.)

O, were that all! I think not on my father,
And these great tears grace his remembrance more
Than those I shed for him.

Discovery: This is extraordinary — perhaps cruel and abnormal — I am crying more now than I did at my father's graveside!

What was he like? I have forgot him...

Discovery: I can't believe this — my father's face, his eyes, the tone of his voice — I can't remember any of it.

... my imagination carries no favour in't but Bertram's.

Discovery: All is truly lost — I have fallen far deeper than I ever realised — my heart and soul ache for only one person — and he is gone.

I am undone; there is no living, none,
If Bertram be away;

Discovery: This is so typical of me — to fall for someone I cannot have and who, if they knew, would surely *never* desire me.

'twere all one
That I should love a bright particular star

And think to wed it, he is so above me.
Discovery: Face it Helena, he is gone — all you have once again is your memories to live on.
In his bright radiance and collateral light
Must I be comforted, not in his sphere.
Discovery: But this won't work — I feel driven, I have little control over what I do or feel — destiny beckons — what to do?!!
The ambition in my love thus plagues itself;
The hind that would be mated by the lion
Must die for love.
Discovery: There is obviously *nothing* to be done — I must needs be consumed by my pain, devoured by my longing. Treasure the fantasy.
'Twas pretty, though a plague,
To see him every hour; to sit and draw
His arched brows, his hawking eye, his curls,
In our heart's table...
Discovery: You made yourself too vulnerable — big mistake — it only ever ends up like this — you cared too much — again.
— heart too capable
Of every line and trick of his sweet favour.
Discovery: You're getting maudlin now — get over it! You have no choice, you can do nothing, get on with your... lonely... life.
But now he's gone, and my idolatrous fancy
Must sanctify his relics.

For the above example I *articulated* each discovery, in a similar way to the inner monologue exercise. The difference here though is that the discovery isn't a verbalised one, but should be expressed through a major and vivid *energy production*. There needs to be a strong and powerful energy impulse produced in *reaction* to the discovery. If you only *think* the discovery you can end up acting purely *between* the lines rather than *on* the line. Better to allow the physical energy produced by the discovery to catapult you *into* the line, making the dialogue not only essential to the experience but also inevitable (see Plates 6 & 7).

When the Countess and Lafew exit, don't *think* about Helena's discovery, intuitively and impulsively *react, physically*. For example, walk away, sink to your knees, turn sharply away from the door. When she discovers she cannot remember her own father, don't *think* how she would feel, *react — create potent physical sensations*. For example, run six metres as if hounded by the discovery, move towards your father's study, placing your hands and forehead against the door. When you discover how impossible your situation is, stand on your toes, reach towards the cosmos, attempt to touch what you cannot possess.

> The consequence of what happens to you must be extreme and profound, otherwise you will give us superficial behaviour.[20]

Through embracing the scene's discoveries in a profoundly *physical* way, the depth and resonance of their meaning become more potent. In the end you may wish to stage Helena's speech standing stock still. But, as with the example we looked at earlier of the photograph album, once the sensation has been experienced, it is forever recorded. These inner impulses will drive the speech and surface in many significant and subtle ways.

By using this exercise I often find that when actors return from their physical exploration of the discoveries and stand to deliver their speech, their acting becomes simple yet clear, their expression more fluid, more lyrical, and their voices often reflect the enormous range they physically experienced moments earlier.

Use *Major Discovery* to unearth the physical impact of the scene's discoveries and therefore events. This will help release your inner impulses and create a dynamic journey for the scene.

EXERCISE 7: Choice of Impact

Explanation The object of this exercise is to entertain the various options for ideas which might fuel each line of text. More importantly, it allows you to focus on the desired *impact* of your lines.

Application We have mentioned before the difference between *sense* and *meaning*: sense being what is stated on the line, meaning being its desired *impact* on the receiver. (If the character is talking to themselves, ascertain what *part* of themselves they are trying to affect — i.e. what aspect of their nature are they attempting to change?) It *is meaning* which directs the audience's attention to the play's interpretation and vision, for the meaning encompasses significance and consequence.

Point of concentration To allow each idea option to be your sole focal point and motivation when you return and commit to the line of text.

ILLUSTRATION 1
In a scene-study class we were working on Sam Shepard's *Fool For Love*. At one point in the text, Eddie, May's lover and half-brother, rises from the table and says to her, 'I'll go'. Upon asking the actor what was the meaning behind his line, he responded, 'Just, I'll go, I guess'. We then looked at some other options:

I'll go and you will be the loser.
I'll go, but tell me to stay.
I'll go, but *don't* ask me to come back.
I'll go; I won't cause any more trouble.
I'll go, and within two hours you'll be on your knees begging me to return.
I'll go, you've really blown it this time, May.
I'll go, and I wouldn't stay if you pleaded with me.
I'll go, but tell me why it should end this way?

Each different idea option shapes the choice and is called a *transaction* — someone or something causing an effect on another. Each *line* becomes a transaction and, as such, must be crafted to achieve its desired result. The options listed above all craft that moment in the play differently and determine the meaning being presented to the audience.

There are 3838 lines in the play *Hamlet*. Every one of them could be counted as a transaction. *Therefore*, each of the 3838 stimuli fuelling the transactions must initially be acknowledged, then processed, and then the actor must release into the play an *energy impulse*. This is the definition of a play: 'an energy moving though time'.[21] As each moment passes through each actor, the play's journey is affected. The energy is either suppressed or supported, diverted or amplified. This process weaves the play's texture and creates the audience's journey. In essence, this moving energy houses the total theatre experience. How this energy is crafted is therefore extremely important.

The *sense* driving the energy impulses becomes the play's *infra-structure*. How each section of this scaffolding is to be *presented to* and *viewed by* the audience depends upon the *meaning* invested in it.

ILLUSTRATION 2

In Barry Levinson's *Diner*, Shrieve confronts his girlfriend Beth about playing his precious record collection. His first line is: 'You've been playing my records again'. Leaving aside for the moment the state of their relationship and what has just occurred, say the above line for sense. That is, Shrieve discovers his records are out of order and states his belief that Beth has been playing them.

Now, with your hand or some paper, cover the ten options listed below. When you're ready, reveal the options one by one, connecting to the idea. Then repeat the line from the play, allowing each individual option to affect the *impact* you wish to create.

Option 1: *I can't believe it — after all I've asked you.* (Repeat line — 'You've been playing my records again'.)
Option 2: *I am so disappointed in you.*
Option 3: *This makes me so angry!*
Option 4: *I'm warning you for the last time.*
Option 5: *It's no big deal, I just need to know.*
Option 6: *This is a joke, right?*
Option 7: *You do this deliberately to upset me.*
Option 8: *I'm trying very hard to control myself at this moment.*
Option 9: *This time I've caught you red-handed.*
Option 10: *This is just not fair.*

Now, evaluate how effective you feel you were in surrendering to each journey the line undertook. To what extent did you monitor and try to achieve the correct 'sound' you felt the line should have had?

The more you allow yourself to *react* to the specific attitude behind each option, the more effective you will be. If your focus falls onto trying to get the 'acting' right, self-consciousness sets in and your pure connection to each idea will be contaminated. If you organically connect to the precise stimulus (cause) and forget about its packaged effect (result) your *reaction* to the stimulus does the acting for you.

Remember: *attitude* is how you feel, *action* is what you do because of it. Each option gives you a clue as to how the character *feels*: i.e. disappointed, outraged, frustrated. You're *reaction* houses your action: i.e. to shock, confront, tease, undermine, shame. *This* is what will propel the scene forward and create drama.

ILLUSTRATION 3

In Shakespeare's *The Winter's Tale*, Hermione is accused by her husband Leontes of adultery. She is arrested and thrown into prison. Upon giving birth to a child believed not to be her husband's, she is brought before the people in the city square to await the Oracle's decision on her fate. She stands facing Leontes who once again accuses her.

HERMIONE: *Sir, spare your threats.*

As we did earlier, cover the options below and reveal them when you are ready. Actors are often reminded not to learn *words*, but *ideas*. With each of the following options, connect to the *idea* it presents and allow this to inform the line:

Option 1: *Please, no more false lies.*
Option 2: *I have no strength left to deny these claims.*
Option 3: *You small-minded fool.*
Option 4: *I know you are misguided and pray for your redemption.*
Option 5: *Do you honestly believe I fear anything of what you say?*
Option 6: *I will not be accused another time!*
Option 7: *If only you knew the destruction you have unleashed.*

When you come to perform your piece the ideas driving the lines will be 'known'. In other words, because of your rehearsal work the ideas will become part of the text, for you can't think one line whilst saying another. The same applies to the inner monologue work we have done. Once the sensations have been fully explored and given their voice, they too become 'known'. They condense and crystallise and become a deeper motivation than can be articulated. When onstage, you feed off this powerful, subterranean source. Once stored, your sense memory retains the galaxy of these sensations. They will be released when triggered by your body experiencing the action and through your verbal commitment to the text. Trust the words, trust the action.

Once you have the process working, ask someone who is familiar with the piece to offer you various options after each line. Don't concern yourself as to their appropriateness; your rehearsal journey will help align the choices that work and this will create your score.

Further Exercises

Listed below are a number of exercises which provide more opportunities for you to discover what may indeed be possible in your chosen scene.

1. Perform your speech within a time limit (45 or 60 seconds) and discover what dynamics emerge and may be appropriate given this sense of urgency.

2. Do your speech at the bedside of a dying person. Allow the thoughts to be informed by this intimate and fragile situation.

3. Build a strong physical activity into your speech: play sport, stack chairs, shadowbox, exercise. Allow these new and active physical impulses to impact upon the ideas.

4. Wash the dishes and imagine the character you are talking to is in the next room. See which words and thoughts become important and in which moments you seek a response.

5. Sit in a chair and close your eyes. Connect to the environment of the speech — the colours, textures, temperature, time, terrain. Allow your personal connections to all the images that build the atmosphere surrounding you to emerge.

6. Build your environment or, if possible, find a place which captures the essence of your speech's experience.

7. Work with another actor: do your speech to them knowing they want to leave the room. This they may begin to do at any time. Use the language to keep their attention.

8. Whilst working with another person, allow them to say, 'And again' anytime they wish a thought was clearer or an image more sharply defined. They may 'And again' you several times on the one line. The 'And again' doesn't request more volume or emphasis, but asks the intention to be clarified, i.e. the meaning and its impact.

9. Stand with your heels and the back of your head resting against a wall. Without moving your arms or head in any way, go through your speech in a whisper. Avoid pushing from the throat — allow your breath to flow easily. Your brain activity will become sharper and the thoughts highly concentrated.

10. As above, but imagine the person you are talking to is twenty-five feet away. Once again, allow your hands, arms and head to remain unengaged — let the thoughts and ideas cover the distance now using voice — watch the words come alive.

11. Choose a beat from your speech: take one thought from your *inner monologue* which you feel drives that beat and repeat it after each line. (see page 59 — *As You Like It*.)

For example, in Act 1, Scene 5 of *Hamlet*, the ghost visits his son. Lines 15 to 20 could be fuelled by the following inner monologue: 'Listen and believe!!!'

Now, repeat this after each phrase of the following text:

Ghost: I could a tale unfold whose lightest word
 would harrow up thy soul, (*Listen and believe!*)
freeze thy young blood, (*Listen and believe!!*)
Make thy two eyes like stars start from their spheres,
 (*Listen and believe!!*)
Thy knotted and combined locks to part,
 (*Listen and believe!!!*)
And each particular hair to stand on end
 Like quills upon the fretful porpentine.
 (*Listen and believe!!!!!!*)

Make up whatever line you feel propels you into the particular essence of the beat. These lines can be as simple as you like: *It's not fair/ She's so beautiful/ I will not stand for it any longer/ Listen to every word I say/ You must believe me/ Come with me now/ Trust in what I say*. Choose an appropriate phrase to repeat, one which informs the text and pinpoints the essential energy driving the beat. This exercise can be enormously stimulating as it invigorates the needs by making them very immediate. It also focuses your attention very much on changing the *will* of the person to whom you are transmitting the ideas — the essence of acting.

All of the examples in this book will hopefully work as triggers to help activate and illuminate your personal process. Each discovery you make will build your craft and lead to a stronger sense of artistry in all you do. Allow yourself to work with courage and conviction. Enjoy the expedition!

To accomplish great things, we must not only act but also dream, not only plan but also believe.

Notes

1) Michael Saint-Denis, *Training For The Theatre*, 1982, Theatre Arts Books, New York.
2) Constantin Stanislavsky, *My Life in Art*, 1980, Methuen, London.
3) Lisle Jones, Head of Theatre, West Australian Academy of Performing Arts.
4) Constantin Stanislavsky, *An Actor Prepares*, 1937, Geoffrey Bless Publishers, London.
5) Constantin Stanislavsky: quoted in Jean Benedetti, *Stanislavsky – An Introduction*, 1982, Methuen, London.
6) C.R. Rogers, 'Towards a Theory of Creativity': included in P.E. Vernon (ed.), *Creativity*, Penguin, London.
7) *ibid.*
8) *ibid.*
9) Stanislavsky, *Collected Works (Vol. IV): Stanislavsky's Legacy*
10) Viola Spolin, *Improvisation for the Theatre*, 1983, Northwestern University Press, USA.
11) *ibid.*
12) *ibid.*
13) Constantin Stanislavsky: quoted in Jean Benedetti, *Stanislavsky – An Introduction*, 1982, Methuen, London.
14) Stephane Mallarme: quoted in Michel Saint-Denis, *Training for the Theatre*, 1982, Theatre Arts Books, New York.
15) Michael Chekhov, *Lessons for the Professional Actor*, 1985, Performing Arts Journal Publications, New York.
16) Arthur Miller
17) Jerzy Grotowski, *Towards a Poor Theatre*, 1968, Methuen, London.
18) Yevgeny Lanskroi
19) Larry Hecht
20) Michael Shurtleff
21) Robert Benedetti

Select Reading List

Brian Bates, *The Way of the Actor*, 1986, Century Books, London.
Robert Benedetti, *The Actor at Work*, 1985, Prentice-Hall, Englewood Cliffs, NJ.
Robert Benedetti, *The Director at Work*, 1970, Prentice-Hall, Englewood Cliffs, NJ.
Patricia Bosworth, *Diane Arbus*, 1984, Avon Books, New York.
Michael Chekhov, *Lessons for the Professional Actor*, 1985, Performing Arts Journal Publications, New York.
Michael Chekhov, *To The Actor*, 1953, Harper and Row, New York.
Shauna Crowley, *The Screen Test Handbook*, 1990, Currency Press, Sydney.
Rollo May, *The Courage to Create*, 1976, Bantam Books, New York.
Michel Saint-Denis, *Training for the Theatre*, 1982, Theatre Arts Books, New York.
Viola Spolin, *Improvisation for the Theatre*, 1983, Northwestern University Press, USA.
Constantin Stanislavsky, *An Actor's Handbook* (edited and translated by Elizabeth Hapgood), 1963, Theatre Arts Books, New York.
P.E. Vernon (ed.), *Creativity*, Penguin, London.

PLATE 7
Uncovering physical impulses behind the thought. Actor, Hugh Jackman.

PLATE 8
The Journey Students at the Actor's Centre in their presentation of *Lulu*. Directed by Ross McGregor. Movement design by Chrissie Koltai.

PLATE 9
'Why bring him here? A storm's coming... He wants to die outside.' W.A. Academy students in Louis Nowra's *The Golden Age*. Directed by Dean Carey.

PLATE 10
'Then have him! Go on, clear out with your soulmate!' Lisa Bailey and Damian Pike as Jeanne and Jim from Betty Roland's *The Touch of Silk*. Directed by Dean Carey

PART THREE

The Monologues

The speeches in the following section offer an extensive selection of audition choices for the actor in training or the actor already working in the profession.

Most are highly suitable for the *General Audition,* where the speech is required to provide range, journey, impact. They present many opportunities for you to explore a wide expressive range.

Other speeches make themselves available for the *Specific Audition*, where you are auditioning for a particular role or type of character. These speeches offer equally strong dynamics but in a more defined and specific form. Their inner landscape may cover less terrain but when fully inhabited, a particular aspect of your abilities will be highlighted and showcased.

You will notice the following icon [★] applied to particular speeches. This denotes that the piece is also suitable for film/TV screen tests where the language needs to be appropriate to this particular audition situation. Still rich in range, these selections promote a more concentrated focus making them ideal for the medium in which they will be viewed. Some are indeed too long, but an edited section would be ideal

I have not classified the speeches under the usual headings of serious, comic, 'serio-comic', and so on. Although such classification might make the speeches easier to locate, I want to avoid influencing your interpretation by predetermining the approach. The scope of a speech is as wide as you wish it.

Please bear in mind that many of the speeches have been edited to create monologues of the right length and so that they give sufficient information to create the 'scene' or context from which they came. When you choose your selections, they should be rehearsed with reference to the complete text. Even if you decide to change the circumstances, please consult the original and complete source. Only should this reference point inform your decisions.

Some speeches are, in fact, too long for the purpose but are valuable to work on without necessarily intending to perform them. How long should a speech be? When conducting a class at The Actors' Centre, Michael Shurtleff, author of *Audition,* said that every speech he has ever *seen* has been too long! I feel that approximately forty-five seconds to one minute for a screen test, and between two and 2½ minutes for a theatre audition, provides a happy medium for all concerned.

LIST OF MONOLOGUES

Australia and New Zealand

Britain and Europe

USA

★= MONOLOGUES SUITABLE FOR FILM/TV SCREEN TESTS.

Cheapside

David Allen

Currency, Sydney 1984

ALICE:

I came down by St Paul's and this bloke was following me and I thought: why not? Cutting Ball, the only brother I'll ever have, deserves a proper wake. So I let the bloke catch up with me. He was a grummidge, straight up from the country. 'Hello, lover,' I said, 'looking for a girl?' It was easy. He was trembling with excitement: he'd never seen a Tyburn hanging before. He wanted a bit of death ecstasy himself. 'How much?' he said. 'What ever you think it's worth, lover,' I said – and I saw him finger his purse, a nice fat one. He'd probably come up to see a lawyer, make a will, order his affairs, bestow largesse and land on his children and relatives, provide for his apple-cheeked wife and himself in their declining years . . .

Didn't ask him where he was from. Wasn't important. All he wanted was a bit of dirt. There was a trugging house just by and I chattered him along there. I knew the Madam, old Dame Bawd from way back, and gave her the wink and the double-talk meaning Plan B. She winked back, acknowledging, and showed us to a room. 'Long time, no see, Alice,' she said. 'Sorry about Cutting Ball.' 'That's life,' I said. 'Isn't it, though?' she said and squeezed my hand and shut the door. So, me and gummidge, into bed, leap, leap. Straight at it – jig-a-jig. When suddenly, ratatat, knocking at the door. 'Who's that? quavers gummidge, shrivelling to a prune. 'The Watch!' comes a deep voice: 'Sent by Justice Brown to search out Jesuits, pick-pockets and any man in delicto with her who is not his lawful wife! 'Oh God!' says gummidge. 'What is it, darling?' I say; 'you ain't a Jesuit, are you? 'No,' he says, 'but you aren't my wife!' 'True,' I says, 'into the closet while I get rid of them –'

[*quietly*] Oh, have you heard it, Rob? It's the one about leaving the coney locked naked in the cupboard and skipping with his purse and clothes . . .

Write it up, Rob. It's a good story . . .

[ALICE *reaches into her skirts and takes out a purse. She empties it onto the table. Coins bounce and roll and clatter to the floor. She gets up and crosses to the table and picks up the baby.*]

Just taking what's mine, Rob. You keep the money and food. They'll keep you going till you write something you can sell.

Dinkum Assorted

Linda Aronson

Currency, Sydney 1989

Act 1 Scene 4

MILLIE:

[MILLIE *fights depression. In her heart she knows* FRANK *is dead, but in a superstitious way she feels that if she can stay happy,* FRANK *will be alive. Nevertheless, her grief and anxiety keep flickering to the surface during her speech.*]

Yes, one fine day – back to Bannakee's! Oh, it's beaut for kids up there. Nothing there, you know, fishing, it's on the ocean . . . There used to be this jetty, half-sunk in the water from when the pearling luggers were there, you know, all rotted away . . . [*Amused*] It used to be the thing for the kids, you know, the dare - how long you'd stay on the jetty as the tide came in . . . [*Bleakly, to herself, forgetting* JOAN] Standing there, the water creeping up your ankles, the birds flying over your head. You'd turn round and all your pals, you know, way off in the distance on dry land. Standing there on this stump, water in front, water coming in behind you.

[JOAN *stares at her.* MILLIE *snaps out of her introspection.*]

Yes, they're doing up the old shipyard there now, building the troop ships. Old Bannakee's won't know itself! That's the war for you, it's brought some changes.

I was such a mess when I first came back to Sydney. Helen wouldn't even talk to me. I got in my husband's car and I drove. I must have been doing seventy, eighty miles an hour. It was night time. I was crying so much I could barely see. And a policeman pulled me over and the tears were streaming down my face. And he asked me what the matter was and I told him about them turning Helen against me and – it was so strange – he got out this thermos-flask of cocoa and we sat on the side of the hill, some enormous hill, drinking cocoa. It was so quiet . . . and pitch dark. Apart from the stars. The sky was full of stars. And suddenly he told me how before the war he'd lived in Melbourne and his wife had gone off with someone because they couldn't have any children and how he'd tried to hunt the lover down and the lover had collapsed and died in the street at the age of twenty-five – this extraordinary story . . . 'I threw my wedding ring into the very depths of the Yarra', he kept saying that. 'I threw my wedding ring into the very depths of the Yarra.'

[*Pause.*]

It's beautiful up here.

After Dinner ★

Andrew Bovell

Currency, Sydney 1989

MONIKA:

I'm fine now. Honestly. Just pretend that nothing happened. It's just that for a moment I thought Martin was still with me and I panicked. Isn't that silly?

I was thinking about what I was going to order when I remembered that I hadn't left anything out for Martin. I thought of him searching through the fridge and not finding a morsel, and I panicked because I hadn't done the shopping. I knew that Martin would be wanting his dinner. I wanted to say something. To tell you that he'd be looking, but I couldn't get it out. It was as though a large piece of phlegm had lodged in my throat and my words couldn't pass it. But then I remembered. Martin wouldn't be wanting his dinner because Martin's not with me anymore. Martin's dead. And the phlegm just slid away.

Poor Martin. If only I was a little quicker. To have held him in my arms before he went. But how was I to know? How was I meant to know he was about to die? Men don't have strokes when they're thirty-eight years old. It wasn't my fault. It wasn't my fault, was it?

Have I told you how Martin died?

We'd finished our dinner. Martin was in the loungeroom watching television and I was in the kitchen doing the washing-up. I'd nearly finished the pots when I smelt this most vile smell. So I put the dog outside. But the smell didn't go away. I searched high and low through that kitchen. Martin couldn't stand unidentified smells. Then I realised that the smell was coming from the loungeroom. I went in, and there was Martin sitting bolt upright in his chair with his nostrils quivering, and the most terrible look on his face. He'd be horrified if I told you, but Martin had lost control of his bowels. Something he normally never would have done. 'Martin, is everything alright?' I said. 'No dear', and they were his last words. He closed his eyes and slid off his chair. The poor man. He was such a clean person when he was alive. So sad that he had to die in such shame. Thank God we didn't have any children. And God knows we tried. Still . . . where would I be now if I had children? Not here, not out on the town having such a good time.

[*Pause as the three women and* GORDON *stare mournfully ahead of them*]

The Girl Who Saw Everything

Alma De Groen

Currency, Sydney 1993

LIZ:

I disagreed with most feminists: I said men didn't really hate women.

I said they were really far more focused on themselves, and the idea women had that men hated them simply made women feel less unimportant.

I wondered if women had been destined from earliest times to be victims: if we were at the mercy of our biology after all.

Manning Clark talked about needing to comfort himself; perhaps that's what historians do – look for comfort amidst the terror.

I became a historian because I was in love with the idea of continuance . . . of something epic and ongoing that I was in service to. But pretty soon it dawned on me that the history of the majority of humanity simply didn't exist. And when you look at the history that *does* exist, you realise it's been defined by one sex. The Renaissance and the Reformation were anything but high points for women. We lost nine million on the witch burnings – for crimes like making penises disappear.

[*Pause*]

But don't bother looking up gynocide in the standard texts. You won't find it. A whole culture is gone. Lost forever. You wipe a lot of memory when nine million people disappear. Anyway why are you asking me? I can't fathom the male psyche. I don't know how I ever imagined I could. I needed. I grabbed. That's all. I mean, Christ, we all need an explanation.

Maybe you don't – but I did.

I was watching a program on rape. None of the rapists viewed the women as objects of anger or hate. What they were angry about was something in themselves, or in society. Not women.

Women were simply there to take it out on. And I thought, if you examine the history that still exists, if you went back as far as that goes, and you looked at the suffering of women, it could seem natural and pre-ordained. You think of primitive man witnessing a breech birth; you think of primitive man whose woman has a prolapse of the womb after childbirth, hanging down like an elephant's trunk between her legs, gangrenous and smelly – and that was common. It happened a lot. Right up until the beginning of this century. Awful things happened to women that couldn't happen to men – so why not make their blood suspect? Why not consider them impure and the object of divine punishment? Why not forbid their menstrual blood to soil the earth on pain of death? Why not consider that she offends heaven and earth? Why not – if you were a Buddhist – create a blood hell especially for women, filled with blood and filth that took 840,000 days to cross and involved 120 different kinds of torture?

[*Pause*]

I said people's lives and destinies are genetically pre-determined. I handed the enemy a stick and said, beat us, that's what we're for. It was irresponsible. It was stupid and a failure of nerve, and now I have to find a way to make up for it.

The Rivers of China

Alma De Groen

Currency, Sydney 1988

Act 2 Scene 8

KATHERINE:

Shall I be able to express, one day, my love of work – my desire to be a better writer my longing to take greater pains? And the passion I feel. It takes the place of religion – it is my religion.

Oh, God! The sky is filled with the sun, and the sun is like music. The sky is full of music. Music comes streaming down these great beams. The wind touches the trees, shakes little jets of music. The shape of every flower is like a sound. My hands open like five petals.

Isaiah – or was it Elisha? – was caught up into Heaven in a chariot of fire *once*. But when the weather is divine and I am free to work, such a journey is positively nothing . . . Cold. Still. The gale last night has blown nearly all the snow off the trees; only big, frozen-looking lumps remain. In the wood where the snow is thick, bars of sunlight lay like pale fire.

I want to remember how the light fades from a room – and one fades with it, is expunged, sitting still, knees together, hands in pockets . . .

I would like to hear Jack saying 'We'll have the north meadow mowed tomorrow', on a late evening in summer, when our shadows were like a pair of scissors, and we could just see the rabbits in the dark.

Daylight Saving

Nick Enright

Currency, Sydney 1990

Act 1

STEPHANIE:

You know what that bastard has done to me now? Yes, I know. I know you said, 'Take it easy, Steph, go easy with this one.' But I thought, no, this is the one, Brendan's the one. I mean, Brendan, that should have been the giveaway, even if I'd missed the Miraculous Medal on the dashboard. But there he was, this vital, vibrant, caring man, who took three months to tell me his marriage was a sacrament, so even though he couldn't live without me, he couldn't live with me. Well, I could live with that, right? I could live with anything. Until tonight. I could live with the guilt, and the clock-watching, and the quick dash for the door to make it home before Bernadette gets back from her

Ecumenical Tae Kwon Do group. I could live with being stood up for a Pentecostal Bushwalk. I can live with Brendan and Bernadette, I mean not live with Brendan because of Bernadette . . . well, because of Brendan, the gutless little Mick turd. I can live with anything but this. You know what he's done, Fliss? You know what Brendan has done? He has given me up for Lent.

Can you believe that? Given me up for Lent. Like I'm a box of chocolates.

That's it. A box of Darrell Lea chocolates, sitting on the shelf, not to be opened till Easter.

I mean, not 'It's over, Steph', nothing that straight-forward. 'I've given you up for Lent, darling.'

Fliss, what am I going to do?

You know, I did think Brendan was it. Intelligent, sensitive, no police record. And after all the ratbags that have come my way. I mean, Ken Willis. You knew Ken.

Well, you remember all that stuff in the papers. Did you know Frankie Snedden?

Ex Manly CID. Took early retirement and went to work for Colonel Rabuka. And best of the lot, Sergei. Sergei Nicolayev, you knew him. Remember the beard and the fur coat?

You don't know anyone, do you?

Sergei was the full Slav bit. Dirty collar, dirty fingernails, straight Stolichnaya for breakfast, the full bit. Black bread and long card games and lots of crying. I was in heaven. Then this old lady turns up looking for Sid. Sid Nichols. It's his Mum from Toukley. His Auntie Iris has died and left him a milk-bar at The Entrance. So he goes off to run the milk-bar at The Entrance. Das Vedanya, Sid. He was the first. But it's not as though I haven't learned. I've learned to look for integrity, sanity and balance. I haven't found them. I've found Ken Willis, the professional cheque-bouncer. Frank Snedden, who brought the poker-machine to Fiji. And now Brendan Kennelly, who has given me up for Lent.

[*She drains her glass.*]

This wine is piss. Of course, all white wine is piss at this hour of the evening.

Away

Michael Gow

Currency, Sydney 1992

Act 3 Scene 2

MEG: I saw the carton. I saw it in the hall.

I saw it. It was near the telephone table, wasn't it?

You saw it too, didn't you? You saw the box sitting there.

You must have. It was sitting next to your vanity case.

Everything else that was in the hall got packed in the car. You did see it.

You were the last one out. You're the one who shuts the door, after you've made sure the stove's off and the fridge has been left open. You saw the carton and you left it there on purpose.

You left it behind.

And you knew what it was. You knew what was in it and you left it there.

Why did you do that?

Why would you do a thing like that?

I want to know why you did it.

Tell me why you deliberately left that box behind.

We have a game we play every year. We sneak presents home, we hide them, we wrap them up in secret even though we can hear the sticky tape tearing and the paper rustling; we hide them in the stuff we take away, we pretend not to see them until Christmas morning even when we know they're there and we know what's in them because we've already put in our orders so there's no waste or surprise. And Dad always hides his in a pathetic place that's so obvious it's a joke and we all laugh at him behind our backs but we play along! You knew what was in that box. You left it behind. I want to know why.

What were you trying to do, what did you want to gain?

Did you want to have something we'd all have to be sorry for the whole holiday? There's always something we do wrong that takes you weeks to forgive.

You have to tell me.

Europe

Michael Gow

Currency, Sydney 1987

Act 4

BARBARA:

Always 'us', 'all of you', 'we', 'them'. Never 'I', 'me', just 'you alone'. Do you ever think of one individual person? Can you look at one human being and see only one human being, or do you have to see millions of others standing behind in a crowd that stretches to the horizon? Germans who are punctual, Frenchmen who all wear berets, Italians all waving their arms in the air, Americans chewing gum? What do all Australians do? How do you see them? I'll tell you what they all do: they beat their heads against a wall crying 'We don't need you. We're as good as you. We are happy with ourselves.' That's all anyone said while I was there. They would tell me over and over and over how independent you all were, how grown up you all have become, how confident, how open, mature, positive, repeating it all constantly like a chant. But it can't be true. No one who is happy needs to repeat, 'I am happy' a thousand times a day to convince himself. All of you are deeply unhappy, as unhappy as everybody else. You are all paranoiacs. You see, I can play that game, I can put you at the front of a crowd and pretend you represent them all. I can go on and on too. I can say that your newness, your freshness, your freedom from tradition attracted my world-weary, neurotic decaying European sensibility. I can say you represent all the things that are missing from my life: romance, laughter, space, clear dazzling light. But I would be talking in cliches. It would have no meaning . . .

[*in a sad, angry outburst*] I missed you so badly! I missed your jokes. I missed your body. I was happy for a week, but human happiness terrifies me. I wanted to stay with you but I couldn't. I didn't want to come home, but I had to. I wish I'd never met you. Being with you again makes me realise how unhappy I really am. I don't want to see you again. And I don't want you to go, ever.

Act 5

BARBARA:

Shhh. You're not supposed to be in here. Shhh. Oh, God, is this the right costume? Is this what I wear first? Can you remember?

[*interrupting*] Of course it is, yes. Yes. This one first, then the green, then, of course, the black. You couldn't tell that I've been drinking alcohol could you? No.

[*She takes a deep breath*]

I only have two more performances of this for a few months. Then the chorus in *Medée.* I hate that too. The girl in the lead can't act. She starts to weep the very second her foot touches the stage. We all cower in the shadows pretending to mourn the children. All these old plays. We do them over and over. We do them this way, we do them that way, we dress them up, we strip them bare, we expose them, we conceal them, we reinforce them, we deny them. And the new plays are just shadows of the old ones. Over and over. Oh, God, why bother doing this? Theatre! It's torture. If only the public knew. If only they would learn something from it. We could go on to something new. But back we go to the next way of doing the same old thing, the new interpretation of the same ancient meaning. One night I *will* give a new interpretation. Sing a song, tell a joke, maybe a story; yes, a true story: avoid the catastrophe completely; no plots, no mysteries, no betrayals. Of course, that would do my career no good at all. Because I can do it all so well.

That's a problem. I am good at it, am I not? [*He nods.*]

Yes. I know I am. But who am I satisfying? The ones in the audience? The ones who already know the ending? I'm not surprising them. There can't be anyone who doesn't know all these stories and how they end: it's always either a wedding or a funeral. And it won't stop everything from going up in smoke. The latest production of *Faust* won't stop the rockets from taking off. But I'll finish the story tonight. I'm such a coward. Aren't I? Oh, yes, I am. But I might take a slightly different route to get to the end. I don't look like I've been drinking do I? Do I look anything like I should?

panic. Douglas, Douglas, Douglas, Douglas, Douglas.

[*She laughs.*]

You've missed the train. Another train. But I've brought you here to make it as painless as I can. I cannot be more humane. It seemed too brutal to let you get on that train. Too . . . too cinematic. There, you see? My head's starting to ache. Now. What? Oh. Too . . . dramatic. The best solution is for you to go the way you came in. In this room. Behind the scenes. I think this shoe is on the wrong . . . Oh, no, that's right. Can you smell alcohol on my breath? Can you?

[*She holds her face close to his.*]

I'm going to drag my body through this classic, yes, and when I come back at the end of this first act, simple: you will be gone. I don't want to know where. I don't want to know what train you're on. You simply won't be here. It's a good idea isn't it? Say 'Goodbye', Douglas.

Now, I go out to the stage. One last glimpse. And I go forever.

[*She goes. Silence. She runs back in.*]

I forgot the book. I have to enter with a book.

[*She rummages around until she finds a book.*]

Say 'Goodbye', Douglas.

The Kid

Michael Gow

Currency, Sydney 1983

SNAKE:

Honestly. I hate this trip. It's always chaos. Always a fight. By the time we get to Auntie Eileen's no one's talking to anyone. I have to do everything. Get the boys ready. Stock up on drinks and Marlboro and chips. Hate it. Won't it be great when we get the money? We'll be happy. We might take over a service station. Dean can fool around with his engines. I'll cook snacks and Pro can man the pumps. I'll have to help him with the change. I'll look back on all this and laugh. Hate it. All the people we end up taking along. Dean always collects someone.

You must have been the first one ever to turn him down. He was that upset. He was driving like a maniac. He just drove over the median strip and back we came. Little turd. Know why he got chucked out of school? Mrs Tucker – guess what Dean called her – was wrapped in him. She used to beat shit out of him, for any reason, no reason, just so she could grab hold of him and whack his bum. One day he'd had enough and he told her to go and see one of the Abo stockmen and he'd fix her up. Poor woman grabbed all the rulers in the room and laid into Dean. He stood up, gave her a right hook and she went down like a ton of bricks. We all stood on the desks and cheered. I reckon Dean would win wars single-handed. The enemy would come to him on bended knees. People will do anything just to get a wink or a smile that says he likes you. Little turd. Foul temper. Lazy. But who cares when it's Dean?

DESIREE:

My father's the Australasian Distribution Manager for The International Church of the Lord.

But people don't care. They're not interested. They don't want to hear. They think religion's just some pretty idiot singing, 'Michael, Row the Boat Ashore'. They can't feel it coming. Or they can and pretend not to.

'But the day of the Lord will come as a thief in the night in which the heavens shall pass away with a great noise and the elements will melt with a fervent heat, the earth also and the works that are therein shall be burnt up.'

Atomic war.

We don't know the exact date. But it's coming.

It's in the Bible.

If you're really interested you can subscribe to God's Survival Kit.

It tells you everything about life. It's the only way to survive what's coming. They're really incredible. They come from

America in these big cartons. I don't suppose you've ever been to America.

Me neither. I'd like to go. It must be incredible. I'd like to see it before Armageddon. But I'll never be able to afford it. I'll have to wait till after. The President supports us. We've got this photostat of a letter he wrote to Dr Patterson thanking him for his best wishes . . . Dad.

He's . . . He's not a hundred per cent committed. He's belonged to lots of different things since he lost his job. He used to be a security guard. They found out he was a member of this anti-migrant group and made fun of him. He bashed one of them up and got the sack. But when he joined The International Church of the Lord I thought he'd finally found it. I mean there's actual living proof in the Bible of the Second World War, the San Francisco earthquake, everything. Even Australia's mentioned. And you can feel it coming, can't you? Just read the papers. Or look at TV. You can feel the end coming. I can't wait. But Dad . . .

He's weak. He's got the answers but he doesn't stick to them. I've never looked back since we joined The International Church of the Lord, but he wavers all the time. He thinks about my mother, I'm sure. Once you accept the Gospel you don't ever have to worry about things, be uncertain. The day our first Kit arrived from America I stopped feeling I had to work everything out for myself. There was this incredible silence in my head. All I have to do now is wait. Sometimes I wake up at night and there's a jet taking off and there's this loud roaring noise. Before I realise what it is I think *now*! It's happening *now*! I wait for the blinding flash of light, that's the first thing. I race out of bed and get Dad and the shotgun.

When you go down into the shelter you have to take a shotgun with you to fight off the others who want to get in with you. It's in the Kit. I race around getting my things and heading for the door. You have to beat the fireball. Then I realise what it is. I go back to bed. But I can't go back to sleep. [*Silence.*] Would you like a kit?

On Top of the World

Michael Gow

Currency, Sydney 1987

Act 1

STEPHANIE:

[*to* BABY, *more gently*] What were you expecting, coming here? You must have been anticipating something. When Marcus offered you this little holiday, what did you expect? What did you see in your mind's eye that made you accept?

Did you expect to go on a holiday with someone you hardly know, hundreds of miles from home, in the home of people you've never met and simply go home and show your mother holiday snaps? Why did you come?

Weren't you afraid to leave home and drive off with someone you hardly knew? You must see things on television. In the papers? Weren't you afraid of being driven down a dead-end track and tied up? Carved up? Left all over the place in garbage bin liners? Kids finding the grisly remains at the dump? Abandoned on that famous stretch of road at night, the police telling you through a loudhailer to get out of the car and run and not to look back and you do and there he is on the roof of the car with a machete dripping blood? Weren't you even a little perturbed?

You like him, don't you?

He is obliging, engaging, sometimes amusing. Not an egotist. But not shy, not awkward. He listens to you and can talk himself, even at length, without boring the listener. He is enormously likeable, physically attractive, calm, still, reserved is probably the word. He is not physically aggressive but can give a sense of protectiveness, of shielding those he likes from stupidity and brutality. Can share confidences, bestowing a sense of specialness, of exclusive intimacy. Can disarm initial hostility by smiling and looking away and flashing his eyes straight back at you, or by winking at you from the other side of the room. Has the ability to leave a person with a feeling of having made a close friend, quite often only after one meeting. He seems a rare creature. He seems . . . good. Am I right?

But he's not good. It's as if my brother has looked upon something usually hidden and it has burned something in him, cauterized some nerve, some link in his nervous system. The basic problem is . . . he tries to fight it . . . but . . . he doesn't care about anything.

Marcus' numbness comes and goes. But it reaches a peak and a very funny thing happens.

He brings home some poor creature, some loser. Like a tame cat bringing home a lizard or a maimed bird because it vaguely remembers what cats used to do. But then it's left to me to hit them with a shovel or flush them down the toilet to continue the metaphor, in order to finish them off. There have been so many. Joanne, Sue, little Stevie, Sammy, Al the Optimist, remember him? Hank the Yank. Gudrun the Beautiful. And Glenda. She lasted the longest. Glenda believed in the power of culture. She was always breaking down and weeping over the Four Last Songs or the Four Quartets or the Four Gospels.

So there you have it. You can stay a few days. We'll send you home. You can fly back if you like.

Act 2

STEPHANIE:

[*very quietly, to* CLIVE] You cannot, cannot, cannot marry her. [*To* BABY] You cannot marry him. Cannot, cannot, cannot, cannot, cannot.

[*To* BABY] I'm sorry for you, but for this family this is the end of the line. We are like the slaves locked in with the dead king, just sitting around waiting for the inevitable. Just go back to your aged mother and do whatever you have to do, make tea and semolina and comb the sparse hair and fluff the pillows and tie up the bedjacket. It's quite hopeless here and we don't need any help. So, go back to your flat.

[*in a sudden rage*] This *is* a prison. You're right. You *are* in prison. I don't care if you never admit life is a bad joke. I don't care if you never once think about death or the size of the universe or how really really tiny your own life is. It doesn't matter. I've got you. I've got you locked up in exactly the kind of life you and your whole generation wanted so badly. It's clean, new, sealed off from the world by a security system. I've got you. You'll never get out. You're stuck here forever. All you've got left is the endless contemplation of how empty all the things you ever hoped for are. And you wasted your time in providing for us, protecting us. The things you kept from us, hunger, fear, cold . . . they got us just the same. You kept them at bay at the front door, but they came around the back and stole us away, like gypsies.

The Boys ★

Gordon Graham Currency, Sydney 1994

NOLA:

Yeah. I just felt like looking out.
[*Pause*]
Huh, what is there you'd want to look at out there?
[*She turns away from the window.*]
That's the worst thing. What this little bloke's goin' to see.
[*She paces up and down, rocking the baby gently.*]
I can't just hide him in a cupboard, can I, sooner or later he's going to go out there into the same world Stevie and Brett and Glenn lived in, and why should he be any different from them? It'd take a lot more than I got to do anything about it.
[*Pause*]
I've had plenty of time to think about it, too, sittin' there in that room starin' at me tummy while it all went on outside. Hah, and you know the first thing I said to meself after the birth? I said,

thank god it's not a girl. 'Cause I'd been thinkin', you know, about what happened to that girl that night. Thinkin' about all sorts of things blokes might do to my girl if she was pretty, and all the things she'd have to cop if she wasn't. Either way she'd lose.

[*Pause*]

I mean I s'pose you can try getting by just being on your own and that, but jeeze they make it tough for you. They make you feel like you're missin' out on so much if you can't go along with it all, can't be the sort of girl who has blokes after her all the time. Lies, that's what it all is, but they make you want to believe it.

[*Pause*]

Even little Stevie, you know, even him, he might seem like a little worm when he's on his own, but when he's with the others, being part of all that, acting the way they do, yeah, there's this kind of energy about him. It's that thing you see all the time, on street corners and outside pubs, and when you see them hanging out of their cars. That energy that holds them together and makes them act the same as each other, whatever they're like inside. It is, it's a kind of energy, and it's full of nothing but evil. And they think they're using it, but no, it's using them! And it'll use this little bloke, too.

[*Pause*]

But there must be something you can do, mustn't there? I mean when he's this young, how could he know anything? So maybe I could . . . I don't know. Make him see what crap it all is, all that stuff he's supposed to believe in.

[*Pause*]

I know what you're thinking. What can a hopeless dag like her do?

Christmas Day

Claire Haywood

Unpublished

KATE:

I didn't go to the hospital. It's Christmas. I hate hospitals. I went into town to look at the lights. They're beautiful tonight. I met an old woman in the park. She said the carols by candlelight were spectacular this year. All the children were like little angels. She was eating her dinner out of a paper bag and everything she owned in the whole world was right there beside her.

We seem to be obsessed with hospitals, don't we? [*Pause*] She's gone, Lou.

[*Kate picks up the doll. She moves towards the television.*] She's finally gone. That's why she came home, see? That's what cats do. It doesn't matter how far away they are, they'll always come home to die. [*Pause*] I understood that tonight. It was so quiet out there. So quiet, I could hear the sound of my own breathing. So quiet and still and empty that I had the feeling I would float away. [*Pause*] I stopped at a house on the way home, to see myself in the window, to make sure I was still there. But the light was on and I could see a family eating. From a big plate in the middle of the table. I wanted to knock on the door, to go inside, to embrace Mum and Dad and Pops and all those relatives I've forgotten and some I've never seen. The cousins and aunts and great uncles who are photos or postcards or dry kisses and flaccid cheeks at weddings and funerals. The ones I have no memory of who never even knew I was born. I wanted to yell: Hey everyone, I'm home! And I suddenly felt this huge wave of relief. As if all the pressure had suddenly gone. [*Pause*] Do you know what the specialist said? He said: you can lead a normal life. Get married, have kids, be perfectly happy, just like that family in the window . . . And then bang! . . . One day the bubble bursts. It's very unusual, he said. But they're finding cases all the time. [*Detached as if she is dissecting the concept*] It starts out as a headache. And then the bleeding begins. Behind the eyes first and then it spreads to parts of the brain. Every attack is an electrical storm that blacks everything out bit by bit until all the lights are gone. [*Pause*] It's in the blood. Passed down from one generation to the next, and down the line it goes.

[*Kate looks out.*]

The fear . . . is like a noise in your head that grows so loud, it deafens you. That's what Pops could hear. It just kept on growing louder and louder . . . [*Pause. She whispers*] I can hear it, Lou.

Caravan

Donald Macdonald

Currency, Sydney 1984

Scene 1

PENNY:

Stop it! Stop it, all of you. I can't stand any more. I really can't.

[*They are so surprised they fall silent. They all look at her.*]

I have had it. Up to here! Do you understand? Every year for four years I have had to endure this holiday. I've had to put up with the heat. I *hate* the heat! The inconvenience, the primitive conditions – there hasn't been a light in the shower for four years. And the *caravan.* Your precious caravan. Parkes, do you know, I *hate* caravans? I hate them. Do you know what I'd like to happen, Parkes? I'd like all the drips to combine into one very big flood and I'd like the caravan to float out to sea. With all of you in it!

You're sorry! Oh yes, you're sorry. For four years I've had the heat, and the caravan, and the children. And Parkes. And it's been *hell!* I thought this year it would be different. I thought . . . with my friends here, I might at least enjoy myself. [*Starting to cry*] But you're *worse*. You're far worse than the children.

We won't go home! We can't go home. It's pouring with rain. We have talked about this holiday for years. We're here and we are stuck with it, and I *insist* that we stay. We have one week to go –

Don't interrupt. And for that week I don't want to hear one nasty word from any of you. Do you hear? Not one word. I want everybody to be nice. I want a week of niceness. All right? No matter what. Or I'll . . . I'll . . . burn the caravan down.

[*She grabs an umbrella and a raincoat and a hat and tries to regain some dignity.*]

I am now going to take a cold shower and then I am going to bed. I don't care where I sleep. Or with whom. As long as there are *no* arguments.

[*She exits into the twilight. Everybody stands transfixed.*]

Sunrise

Louis Nowra

Currency, Sydney 1983

IRENE:

She loves him very much.

One day I hope she'll go back to Africa and see him as he really is, a marvellous scholar who's gone troppo –

He became so immersed in the language and culture of the people he studied that he became one of them. He used to take Venice to fetish markets –

God, they're disgusting; putrid smells. Monkey heads, dog's teeth, gecko skins –

He loved buying them. As souvenirs, he said; but he believed in their powers –

Once, when I was in Paris, he took Venice to a tribe who wanted her to help break the drought, because she was white-skinned and blonde like their spirit ancestors –

Venice was covered in black grease. Geckos and a goat were slaughtered and their blood poured over her.

All the while Alex took pictures. You can see Venice's eyes in the photographs – such terror, such incomprehension! I'll never forgive him for that. She was only seven.

And she still loves him more than she loves me. Venice has no barriers between her and life. She's like a sponge that soaks up everything.

She's a world I'm not allowed entry into.

Even when she was born she had distant eyes [*Smiling*] But what can you expect coming from this background –

I don't know what I'm going to do with her, David. Sometimes I think she's a normal fourteen-year-old and then . . . other times I know she's *touched*.

Hotel Sorrento

Hannie Rayson

Currency, Sydney 1992

Act 2, Scene 12

MEG:

The problem with loyalty is that you can keep on and on, living a lie. And you don't even know you're doing it.

[TROY *doesn't understand.*]

I don't know whether you'll be able to make sense of any of this. But I'll tell you anyway. It's not fair otherwise.

[*Pause*]

For quite a long time, I was very much in love with him. Your Dad. I never admittted it. In fact I only admitted it to myself when I was half way through my book. He was such a wonderful man. He was loving and warm and generous. And so funny. He used to make us laugh. Hil and me. We'd be on the floor, holding our stomachs. Absolutely weak with laughter.

[*She smiles at the memory.*]

He was also very sensual. Very affectionate. For those last two years before he died, I thought that he wanted to have an affair with me. I'd got it into my head that he was quite infatuated. And maybe he was. A little bit. But I was resolved that nothing could happen. He was married to my sister. You don't do that. Still, I think if I'm honest . . . I did want something to happen. Anyway that night, I was staying with Dad. The phone rang about midnight and it was Gary. He said he had to meet with me urgently. Somewhere private. So I agreed to meet him on the pier. I got there first and I waited and after a while he came walking up the pier huddled in his jacket. It was very cold and he stood there trying to roll a cigarette and his hands were shaking. He was really agitated. He said, 'Meg, I've done something really stupid'. He was finding it impossible to get the words out. And then he said it, 'I'm having an affair with Pippa'.

[*Long pause.* MEG *daren't look at his face.*]

I'm sorry Troy, I'm sorry it's so shoddy.

[*Silence*]

I asked him whether Hil knew and he said he didn't think so . . . and then he asked me what he should do. And I said 'End it obviously', and I turned my back and walked down the pier and I never saw him again. I just turned my back. And that was the night he drove his car into a tree. A month later I went to England . . .

[*Long silence*]

You must never think he did it on purpose. It was an accident. I don't know what your mum knows, Troy. She thinks it was me I think.

[TROY *puts his head on* MEG'*s shoulder. She puts her arm around him.*]

I'm sorry Troy.

Act 2, Scene 14

MARGE:

'Yearning for something that she could not name'

[MEG *smiles at the reference to her book.*]

My relationship to this place has changed so much since reading *Melancholy.*

[*Pause*]

I didn't get the chance to talk about it with you yesterday, but what I wanted to say was that reading *Melancholy* was just like the experience I had when I first read Helen Garner. I remember reading *Monkey Grip* and thinking, 'This is the place where I live and I've never seen it like this before'. It was as though she'd given me the summer in the inner suburbs. Like it hadn't existed until I read her book. And all of a sudden, everything became meaningful – going down to the Fitzroy pool – Aqua Profunda – and walking to the shop on one of those hot evenings and smelling the asphalt. Watching those young women in their cotton dresses riding their bicycles through the park. She gave it to me. She gave it life.

I feel the same about Sorrento. It's not just the pretty little place that I come to every weekend for a bit of R & R. Not any more. I've started to feel that I *need* to come here. I take that walk often you know – from the back beach across the headlands towards Portsea. And I think I've found the place Grace calls 'The Great Rock'. '. . . perched on the fartherest point, with the steepest fall, a place for glorious departure.'

[MEG *smiles.*]

It's so wild, with the wind and the surf smashing around over the rocks. Way down there at the foot of the cliffs. I feel as though you've awakened something in me. It's like a yearning, a real yearning . . . to . . . feel again.

[*Pause*]

One closes down on one's passions so much. I suppose I always used to choose the sheltered spots . . . [like Helen] but not . . . I feel this urgency . . . to be part of it all, part of the expanse.

[MEG *is deeply touched by* MARGE*'s outburst.*]

I always used to paint with watercolour you know, but now I've started to use oils.

Act 2, Scene 16 ★

HILARY:

'Troy, listen to me. You didn't see anything. By the time you looked back there was nothing there. If there was something, Troy . . . if he'd been calling you, or waving his arms . . . if you'd seen anything, you would have gone back in there. I knew you would. And not because you're brave – even though you are – you're the bravest kid I know. But you would have done it, Troy. Just on instinct. I know that more than I know anything in the whole world. But you didn't, you see, because there was nothing there. There was only the sea.

[*Pause*]

One day, Troyby, one day . . . we'll walk along the back beach and we'll look out at the sea and we won't be frightened by it any more. We'll say, 'This is what happened'.

[*Pause*]

We don't know why, but what we do know is that it didn't happen to you and it didn't happen to me. We're the lucky ones.

[*Pause*]

We've got a lot to feel sorry for – you and me. God knows. But I'm buggered if I'm gonna go under. And I'm not gonna let you either.

Hate

Stephen Sewell

Currency, Sydney 1988

CELIA: Show me, Michael! Show me how to live!
I know he's alive!
I love him!
I don't know how, but I do!
[*Pause.*]

I love his power and his strength: I love the clarity of his mind; I love his lack of pettiness, his drive; I love his vision, his unflinching gaze; I love his willpower. There's nothing I wouldn't do for him. I love him.

If he's so mad, so's the world. I want it, Michael. I want its fury to possess me.

I'm worth nothing.

I'm a lie.

I never loved Geoffrey; I can see that now. All it ever was was just one more battle with Father.

As soon as I had him I could see everything Dad had said was true. He was a fool, he was a coward; he was everything Father wasn't and I hated him. I hated him so much I'd find myself daydreaming he'd been killed in a car accident; stabbed, bashed. I wanted him dead. And then he just slipped away, somehow slipped out of my consciousness and I forgot he even existed. One day I found myself in bed with another man and I felt nothing: no remorse, just empty, the sheets of the bed and this stranger next to me, touching me as if he owned me, the light through the window. Who was he? The first man? The tenth? How many men had I slept with? Who were they? Where do all these men come from? What do they want? I hated him!

[*Thunder rolls.*]

He was inside me and I hated him; in my thoughts, in my dreams; even the way I held a teacup reminded me of him. And then I realised there was nothing I could do, nothing I could be, to ever get away from him.

[*She crosses the stage, more composed.*]
Look at him, look at him through the windows: his dark land; his anger. Look at how he scoured his soul, razed it to the ground and scorched it, possessed it like an animal and ridden it till it screamed in anguish. I love him.

Sisters ★

Stephen Sewell

Currency, Sydney 1991

Scene 7

SYLVIE:

It wasn't anything – It didn't mean anything – We'd been going out together – Going out? – Seeing one another – for six months – He was married, so there was nothing in it – I don't know why I did it – Why do you do these things? I'd been involved with married men before and it was always a disaster; but then it starts again and you think it'll be alright – It was stupid, it was just stupid – Anyhow, the end came and he said he couldn't stand it anymore; and that's when it happened – I got pregnant – Can you imagine that? I didn't even want to be pregnant – Not then, not with him.

I knew the night it happened – I knew the moment it happened – The desperation, the sadness – All my life seems to be arrivals and departures – I wanted him so much, then, at that moment – I never wanted him to leave – I wanted him there, inside me, forever . . .

I don't know – I didn't think. I thought this time it could be different.

This time, anytime – What happens to me? I don't know – Somehow the light changes, the air seems to vibrate and it just feels as if everything is going to be alright – Do you understand what I'm saying?

Before you fall in love: your senses become sharper, laughter is sweeter – It's the anticipation, even before you're aware of it; someone triggers something inside you; it might be a glance, the way they look at you out of the corner of their eye, and before you know it, everything you're doing is seductive; you're seducing them; you don't even know who it is yet, at that table, in that room; but you're seducing them, enjoying the pleasure of a moment that doesn't yet have a name and that might pass into nothing without any guilt and no commitments but sits like a seed in your mind till you see that person again, and you know it is him and that something secret has passed between you; that each of you now has a piece of the other lying like a dark hand on your soul; and then the guilt begins, and the need burns and the air around you darkens again till you have that next delicious moment when you can take him into you and begin to live again.

The Man on the Mountain

Irene M. Summy Univ. of Qld Press, Brisbane 1970

Scene 1

WOMAN:

Perhaps if I explained the situation, you'd understand it better. You'd see my point. You'd realize how deeply I've been wronged. But I can see in your eyes that you're already against me. You admire him. Even though you're angry that he stopped you from climbing the mountain, you can't help admiring him. You think he's clever, don't you? And you'd like to be like him. Admit it. You respect him. Isn't that true? The people in the village are just the same. I've talked to them for hours and tried to present my case, but they do not have time to listen or to understand. They walk away, as though I did not exist. They ignore me. They yawn in my face, and some of them even laugh.

You've no idea what I've suffered. I – who've had no experience with suffering at all. The people down there are prepared to suffer. They are taught resignation from the moment they leave the womb. They are born to suffer and come to accept and expect it as part of living. Life is suffering and bliss comes afterwards in heaven. Without suffering no bliss. They cannot escape their suffering. They cannot move a foot without hurting or being hurt. And yet their feet keep moving with lunatic determination. I've watched them from my peak for years and marvelled at their stupidity. [*Pause.*] Marvelled, I said. NOT pitied, for each had the power to change his life, to rise above it, but none ever did. If a wall could not be moved, or scaled, they stuck with it, pleading with it, shouting at it, kicking it, banging at it with their fists, knocking on it with their heads, until they were battered and bleeding, and still the wall did not budge, and still they would not quit and go away.

But I was different. Suffering never touched me. I'd studied it as children study *Othello* at school without experience or any concept of jealousy.

You are a compassionate man. I can see that. A true humanitarian. You'll understand the injustice of it all. And since you insist, I'll tell you the story and let you judge for yourself, if my sufferings are justified or not.

It all began a long time ago, when I was just a little girl. My parents brought me here to climb the mountain, at a time when my father was greatly distressed. His mother had died the week before, and he'd cried for several nights thereafter, and still did. Such a harsh, ugly sound, the sound of a man's grief, if one has never heard it before. His eyes were still red from weeping, the day we climbed the mountain, and I was careful not to look at him, but looked at the view instead. I'd never before seen the world from above, seen it in its true perspective with reality receding into a mist of insignificance, while the huge grown-up world turned into a toy land of make-believe.

Diving For Pearls

Katherine Thomson

Currency, Sydney 1992

Act 1

BARBARA:

They're changing the name of the beach, to fit the hotel. Why not, they've got the money. Why shouldn't they? 'City Beach'. City Beach. It doesn't make sense anyway. Listen to this, see all those windows, not one single one of those windows has any kind of view of the steelworks. Or the State Engineering Works. Or anything revolting. Design. 'What industry?', you'd say up there. 'I can't see anything. Whack some more champagne in the orange juice'. All the beach and up the back of the escarpment. I mean that's more or less rainforest that escarpment. Rainforest! Rainforest's fashionable, always going on about it. It's a goldmine and why not? Why shouldn't we have a goldmine here? Japs see all that sand, they won't be able to stop themselves. Yanks'll be flying here direct.

We think we don't deserve this, that's the problem. The entire city's got an inferiority complex. You know what international means? They know how to make a go of it and they know what the fuck they're doing. A lovely pink palace.

And think how many people they're gonna need to run it. They'll have to take some locals, Den. The Labour Council'll make them take some locals. But what calibre of person are they going to get? They won't be wanting Miss Macedonia from Kentucky Fried or Doris from Dapto who lost her finger in the tin plate mill. I don't want to be mean but they'll be after a different class of person. And when those cranes come off that roof and they put a bathplug in every room and wrap all those toilets in all that white ribbon like they do – who do you reckon's going to be there? Part of the team. They're having teams. I'm not going to be distracted from this, Den.

I'm not stupid. I've gone into it. I know my age. You don't go for waitressing or behind the bar, women my age are hostesses.

Here's your table, where's your waiter, here's the conference room. Have a nice conference. I know I'm rough around the edges, I'm not stupid, you might think I am.

I know you have to look the part. Like you were eating croysants before anyone else had heard of them. [*She presents him with some brochures.*] You can do anything these days. Well you have to. Now this course, or – [*She takes a quick look at the brochures.*] I suppose you'd say diploma – it's not only for models. Or teenagers. Personally tailored to fit your requirements. It's not one of those crummy ones. It's a proper Academy.

[*Pause*]

A brand new start.

It's not modelling. I'm not stupid.

[*Pause*]

I haven't got the money.

[DEN *looks up at her.*]

Well you knew that. I've never made a secret of that. I had bloody Barry frittering it away. Never have a joint cheque account. And I was never bonus-hungry, just run up my quota. Why go over, it's exactly what they want.

[*Pause*]

It's practically full-time.

[*Pause*]

I've got an artist's impression of that hotel on my fridge. You know what I mean?

[BARBARA *is starting to realise that he may not pay.*]

I wouldn't ask you but it's an investment.

I just knew something was going to hit me.

[*Sound of a band in the distance.*]

Miners' Federation Band.

I always like to cry whenever I see a brass band.

[*Nearly in tears, she starts to take the brochures out of* DEN*'s hands.*]

[*excited*] Not them lot. That lot's so old, every time they go out marching someone else drops dead. They've hardly got any instruments left, it's all done with tape-recorders. [*To* DEN]

Definitely no tuba. [*The brochures*] Have a look? Think about it, eh?

[*Pause*]

Everywhere I've ever worked, they check your bag when you leave for the day. They wouldn't do that there.

[*She has been smoking a cigarette. As she turns she looks up at the hotel. She decides to give up smoking.*]

[*excited that* DEN *has not said 'no' and stamping out her cigarette.*] Right, that's the last one. Dead give-away, aren't they? Common. Lucky thing I never had my ears pierced.

[*The band continues to play in the distance.*]

A Handful of Friends ★

David Williamson

Currency, Sydney 1976

SALLY:

Ron Carroll came to him two days later offering straight cash. The agent's kicking himself. I've steered you into the best film buy you've ever had and now you want to toss me aside, and don't think I don't know the reason. Sheer pragmatism. Now you're onto a big budget you're going to get yourself some overseas star.

You're just going to keep your options open until the last minute, aren't you? If I was ninety-nine percent right for the part and little miss ninety-nine point two came along you'd ditch me without a minute's hesitation.

I see. It's all right if I exercise my skills and judgement to get you the option but now I've done my bit I can go to hell. You've got the power now and you're going to use it.

So now it's lick my boots or else. Yes, yes, yes. I can see where I went wrong. I should have been born a man and have had a father who was a baker or a grocer or whatever in the hell he was, and he would have told me to be hard working and diligent and to have direction in my life, and I wouldn't have wasted so much time tramping through Europe and Africa and Asia seeing what the world was all about, loafing about in the little cafes . . .

No! I would've stayed at home and become qualified and become and sales manager of the fastest growing ladies underwear manufacturer in the country, and even though I found this vocation quite spiritually enriching, my basic driving ambition might have led me on from there to apply for a sales manager job in a television company which I would have taken up after a tearful farewell from my old ladies underwear chums who might have been so moved as to present me with a beautiful leather briefcase filled with silk panties, for they would surely not be without wit and humour. Then by a combination of diligence, industry, bullying and back-stabbing I might have wormed my way into production and got to direct and produce my very own soap opera, the first of many such gifts of mine to the culture of the nation.

After producing and directing this epic for three years I might have even got up enough courage to launch out and make a movie. Perhaps I would have even been lucky enough to meet a woman who urged me to *keep* making them and who was intelligent enough to talk to me about scripts and casting and which scenes to drop and which scenes to retain . . .

However I'm not a male and my father wasn't a grocer and I'm not hard working, diligent, sly, opportunistic, persistent and deceitful and I'm rather glad because that self-righteous, small town, grocer's-son-makes-good, self-congratulatory, paranoic manner of yours makes me sick.

[MARK *glares at* SALLY *with barely contained fury*.]

Go on. I'm an arrogant bitch. Whjy don't you say it?

[SALLY *picks up a knife lying next to a platter of cheeses and hands it to* MARK.]

Go on. Carve me up. That's what you'd like to do, isn't it? I'm arrogant. Carve me up. Here. Right across the throat.

SALLY:

Jill, most of it isn't even true! I'm getting that film role because Mark thinks I'm the best person for it. He wouldn't give it to me if he didn't. He's the most utterly ruthless man you can imagine. I could rant and scream until doomsday and it wouldn't make any difference. If he found an actress who was half of one percent better for the role he'd get rid of me without a moment's hesitation. He's admitted it.

My performance is good in his last film, Jill. Mark wouldn't use me again if it wasn't.

[SALLY *moves across and takes the magazine from where* JILL *has placed it and begins to read.*]

"And while one can only admire the audacity of Marshall in casting his wife Sally as a sensitive, tactful and loyal academic's wife, this is one time when casting against type has come unstuck. And how." Jill, I may not be as sensitive and tactful and loyal as you'd want me to be but you've made me sound like a monster. [*Reading again*] "Attraction to other people is often more a matter of style than content, and what Sally lacked in content she surely made up for in style." Jill, you've made me sound like an absolute monster.

Mark wants to sue you and he's got grounds, but the only thing that I want to know is why you did it? I can't understand it. We were sitting here laughing together on this couch only a week ago. Mark really wants to sue you.

You realise that I can't possibly do the part in *Richard Mahony* now, don't you? I'd be subjected to utter ridicule. You do realise what you've done to me, don't you?

Is it true that you organised getting me fired from the magazine? Did you really go to Iris Burke?

I'm a blind food, aren't I? I was naive enough to think that you would be pleased to have me on the staff because you all knew I was a good journalist. The only reason Iris Burke hired me was because I was good. I got better interviews out of better people than anyone else around and I assumed you'd be big enough to admit that to yourselves and accept it without conspiring behind my back. And all that garbage about sleeping with people to get the interviews is just so much crap. Sure I slept with a few, and so did you if I remember correctly and I still managed to get better interviews. It's just pure spite, Jill, and I've had enough of it. I've had it all my life. When I was twelve a girl I'd known for three years came up to me in the classroom and started stabbing me with a compass screaming: "She thinks she's bloody fantastic, Miss." I'm just sick of that sort of envy, Jill, and the last person I expected it from was you. I'm sorry I didn't ring you after I moved in with Mark but I always sensed there was something wrong when I was living here . . .

You must have felt terribly smug seeing me reduced to a nonentity and knowing you were responsible for it.

The Prime of Miss Jean Brodie

Jay Presson Allen

Samuel French, New York 1969

Act 2

BRODIE:

I will not resign and you will not dismiss me, Miss Mackay. I will not allow you to exercise me on your warped compulsion to persecute! I will not be slandered, hounded - you will *not* use the excuse of that pathetic - that *humorous* document to bully and blackmail me into resigning. Mr. Lowther - you are witness to this. Miss Mackay has made totally *unsupported* accusations against my good name. And yours. If she has one authentic shred of evidence, just *one*, let her bring it forth! Otherwise, if any further word of this outrageous calumny reaches my ears, I shall sue. I shall take Miss Mackay to the public courts, and I shall sue the trustees of Marcia Blaine School if they support her. I will not stand by and allow myself to be crucified by a woman whose *fetid* frustration has overcome her judgement! If scandal is to your taste, Miss Mackay, then I shall give you a *feast*!

I am a teacher! I am a teacher! First! Last! Always! Do you imagine for one instant that I will let that be taken from me without a fight?

I have dedicated, sacrificed my *life* to this profession. And I will not stand by like an inky little slacker and watch you rob me of it. And for *what* reason? *For jealousy*. Because I have the gift of claiming girls for my own. It is true that I am a strong influence on my girls. Yes! I am proud of it! I influence them to be aware of all the possibilities of life. Of Beauty, of Honor, of Courage. I do not, Miss Mackay, influence them to look for ugliness and slime where they *do not exist.* [*Takes a deep breath.*] My girls will be coming back from recreation so I shall return to my classroom. They will find me composed and prepared to reveal to them the succession of the Stuarts. [*Strides toward the door, turns.*] And on Sunday I shall visit Mr. Lowther at Cramond. We are accustomed, bachelor and spinster, to spend Sundays together in sailing, in walking the beaches, and in the pursuit of music. Mr. Lowther is teaching me the mandolin. Good day, Miss Mackay.

Absent Friends

Alan Ayckbourn

Penguin, London 1981

Act 2

DIANA:

[*quietly at first*]: When I was a little girl, you know, my sister Barbara was very jealous of me because Mother bought me this coat for my birthday . . .

I'd seen it in the window of this shop when I walked to school. It was red with one of those little collars and then trimmed round the neck and the sleeves. I used to pass it every day. They'd put it on this window dummy. A little child dummy. It was a really pretty dummy. Not like some of them. A proper face. It had very very blue eyes and sort of ash coloured hair, quite short and it was standing in the middle of this sort of false grass. I wanted that coat so much. And Barbara used to say, you'll never get Mother to buy you that. But I did. And on my birthday, I put it on and I felt, oh, so happy you can't imagine. And then we were all going for a walk and we were just going out and I happened to catch sight of myself full length in the mirror in the hall. And I looked like nothing on earth in it. I looked terrible.

I wanted a red one especially. Because I had this burning

ambition, you see, to join the Canadian Royal Mounted Police.

People used to say 'You can't join the Mounted Police. You're a little girl. Little girls don't join the Mounted Police. Little girls do nice things like typing and knitting and nursing and having babies.' So I married Paul instead. Because they refused to let me join the Mounted Police. I married him because he kept asking me. And because people kept saying that it would be a much nicer thing to do than . . . and so I did. And I learnt my typing and I had my babies and I looked after them for as long as they'd let me and then suddenly I realized I'd been doing all the wrong things. They'd been wrong telling me to marry Paul and have babies, if they're not even going to let you keep them, and I should have joined the Mounted Police, that's what I should have done. I know I should have joined the Mounted Police. [*Starting to sob.*] I want to join the Mounted Police. Please . . .

[*She starts to sob louder and louder till they become a series of short staccato screams.*]

Revengers' Comedies

Alan Ayckbourn Faber & Faber, London 1991

IMOGEN:

Henry, I'm sorry, I can't go away and live with you in a bedsit. Not with two children. I love my home, too, actually. So do the kids. It's paradise for them. What's more, it's mine. I don't see why I should just give it all up and leave it for Anthony. If anyone's going, it's him. So there.

It's a dead marriage. The last rites have long been read. I know that. You know that. But unfortunately Anthony doesn't. He will not let go. He doesn't really want me any more but he won't let me go. Why? I don't know. The children, of course. He's fond of them. And, whatever else, I'm very useful to him and he'd find it extremely hard to get another woman to run things the way I do for absolutely no thanks at all. I don't think either Karen Knightly or Daphne Teale would do what I do for him.

[*Sighing*] You're right. I should just let the whole place go to pot. Let the pigs starve, the chickens get bunged up with eggs, the cows fill up with milk and burst . . . I don't know. Why do I clean the kitchen floor every single evening once the kids have gone to bed? I don't know . . . Yes, I do know, actually. Because I can't bear wading through filth, that's why. I can't bear bits of old bread and Marmite glued to my instep. God, I loathe Marmite. [*Pause.*] I'm sorry. I don't make it very easy, do I? [*Pause.*]

God, I'm in such an *awful* state, I don't know what's the matter with me. It's much too early for the change, isn't it? I do hope so. I went to the children's concert the other day, you know. It was absolutely God-awful. I mean *frightful*. You've no idea. And our two were just so embarrassingly bad, it wasn't true. And I sat there crying my eyes out. As if I was watching some wonderful, brilliant opera. Or *King Lear* or something. There they were, all standing in a line singing 'Nick-nack Paddiwack' and me in floods of tears. God, it was so dreadful . . .

[*She trails off, unable to continue.* HENRY *holds her gently.*] I'm sorry. I'm such a dreary person to be with. I wouldn't blame you if you went and found someone terribly fat and jolly . . .

Victory

Howard Barker

John Calder, London 1983

Act 2, Scene 1

DEVONSHIRE

I do feel clean here. I do feel clean. The wind off the estuary.

And the low cloud racing, and the grey flat water, the thin surf on the mudbank, really it is better than a marine landscape by Mr Van Oots and in any case I don't think I like sex. [*Pause. She breathes.*] Oh, this is pure, this is absolute life, I never felt so whole and so completely independent, this is the third letter in a week begging me back and in verse too! All very flattering but really it is pure dick, a woman should never forget a poem is actually dick, should she? . . .

To look at me you'd think she knows no pain, now, wouldn't you? I'm sure you say that, privately. Admit you say that. . . .

Oh, you do, you do! Her lovely this, her lovely that, you do, of course you do, you think I have no agonies. But there are pains and pains, aren't there? . . .

I am twenty-four and have miscarried seven times. That is wicked, isn't it, of God? . . .

It is particularly cruel because I care for men. Last week I thought the floor of my body was being was being bitten out, by rats, by dogs, I thought my whole floor going, have you had that? . . .

I cannot keep a child in, absolutely cannot, yet I conceive from a look, what is the matter with God, my womb is only fit for a nun, is that His way, do you think? I will die from one of these drops. I would keep away from dick if I could, but you cannot be as a good as I am, looking as I do, and keep away from them, can you? I am trying to appreciate views instead, but he writes so beautifully, my rump, my rump, he goes on about, keeps him awake at nights, my whispering hair and so on, I go back tonight, I know all poems are dick but I go back, I will die of him, it is silly but he makes me feel alive. What's your advice? I believe in asking strangers for advice, you cannot trust your friends, I believe in essence all your friends wish you dead. Say yes or no.

Bed Among the Lentils ★

Alan Bennett

From *Talking Heads,*
BBC Books, London 1990

SUSAN:
When I woke up it was dark and Geoffrey'd gone out. I couldn't find a thing in the cupboard so I got the car out and drove into Leeds. I sat in the shop for a bit, not saying much. Then I felt a bit wanny and Mr Ramesh let me go into the back place to lie down. I must have dozed off because when I woke up Mr Ramesh has come in and started taking off his clothes. I said, 'What are you doing? What about the shop?' He said, 'Do not worry about the shop. I have closed the shop.' I said, 'It's only nine. You don't close till eleven.' 'I do tonight,' he said. I said, 'What's tonight?' He said, 'A chance in a million. A turn-up for the books. Will you take your clothes off please.' And I did.

SUSAN:
Mr Ramesh has evidently been expecting me because there's a bed made up in the storeroom upstairs. I go up first and get in. When I'm in bed I can put my hand out and feel the lentils running through my fingers. When he comes up he's put on his proper clothes. Long white shirt, sash and what not. Loincloth underneath. All spotless. Like Jesus. Only not. I watch him undress and think about them all at Evensong and Geoffrey praying in that pausy way he does, giving you time to mean each phrase. And the fan club lapping it up, thinking they love God when they just love Geoffrey. Lighten our darkness we beseech thee O Lord and by thy great mercy defend us from all perils and dangers of this night. Like Mr Ramesh who is twenty-six with lovely legs, who goes swimming every morning at Merrion Street Baths and plays hockey for Horsforth. I ask him if they offer their sex to God. He isn't very interested in the point but with them, so far as I can gather, sex is all part of God anyway. I

can see why too. It's the first time I really understand what all the fuss is about. There among the lentils on the second Sunday after Trinity.

SUSAN:

I stand up and say, 'My name is Susan. I am a vicar's wife and I am an alcoholic.' Then I tell my story. Or some of it anyway. 'Don't pull any punches' says Clem, my counsellor. 'Nobody's going to be shocked, believe me love, we've all been there.' But I don't tell them about Mr Ramesh because they've not been there. 'Listen, people. I was so drunk I used to go and sleep with an Asian grocer. Yes, and you won't believe this. I loved it. Loved every minute.' Dear oh dear. This was a real drunken lady.

So I draw a veil over Mr Ramesh who once, on the feast of St Simon and St Jude, put make-up on his eyes and bells on his ankles, and naked except for his little belt danced in the back room of the shop with a tambourine.

'So how did you come to AA?' they ask. 'My husband,' I say. 'The vicar. He persuaded me.' But I lie. It was not my husband, it was Mr Ramesh, the exquisitely delicate and polite Mr Ramesh who one Sunday night turned his troubled face towards me with its struggling moustache and asked if he might take the bull by the horns and enquire if intoxication was a prerequisite for sexual intercourse, or whether it was only when I was going to bed with him, the beautiful Mr Ramesh, twenty-six, with wonderful legs, whether it was only with him I had to be inebriated. And was it, asked this slim, flawless and troubled creature, was it perhaps his colour? Because if not he would like to float the suggestion that sober might be even nicer. So the credit for the road to Damascus goes to Mr Ramesh, whose first name turns out also to be Ramesh. Ramesh Ramesh . . .

But none of this I say. In fact I never say anything at all. Only when it becomes plain to Geoffrey (and it takes all of three weeks) that Mrs Vicar is finally on the wagon, who is it gets the credit? Not one of Mr Ramesh's jolly little gods busy doing everything under the sun to one another, much like Mr Ramesh.

Oh no. It's full marks to Geoffrey's chum, the Deity, moving in his well-known mysterious way.

Mr Ramesh sold his shop. He's gone back to India to fetch his wife. I went down there on Sunday. There was a boy writing Under New Management on the window. Spelled wrong.

Single Spies

Alan Bennett

Faber & Faber, London 1989

CORAL:

Listen, darling. I'm only an actress. Not a bright lady, by your standards. I've never taken much interest in politics. If this is communism I don't like it because it's dull. And the poor dears look so tired. But then Australia is dull and that's not communism. And look at Leeds. Only it occurs to me that we have sat here all afternoon pretending that spying, which is what you did, darling, was just a minor social misdemeanour, no worse – and I'm sure in certain people's minds much better – than being caught in a public lavatory the way gentlemen in my profession constantly are, and that it's just something one shouldn't mention. Out of politeness. So that we won't be embarrassed. That's very English. We will pretend it hasn't happened because we are both civilized people.

Well, I'm not English. And I'm not civilized. I'm Australian. I can't muster much morality, and outside Shakespeare the word treason to me means nothing. Only, you pissed in our soup and we drank it. Very good. Doesn't affect me, darling. And I will order your suit and your hat. And keep it under mine. Mum. Not a word. But for one reason and one reason only: because I'm sorry for you. Now in your book . . . in your *real* book . . . that probably adds my name to the list of all the other fools you've conned. But you're not conning me, darling. Pipe isn't fooling pussy. I *know*.

East

Steven Berkoff

John Calder, London 1982

Scene 7

SYLV:

I for once would like to be a fella, unwholesome both in deed and word and lounge around one leg cocked up and car keys tinkling on my pinky. Give a kick* at talent strolling and impale them with an impertinent and fixed stare . . . hand in Levi-Strauss and teeth grinding, and that super unworrisome flesh that toys betweeen your thighs, that we must genuflect and kneel to, that we are beaten across the skull with. Wish I could cruise around and pull those tarts and slags whose hearts would break as he swiftly chews us up and spits us out again . . . the almighty boot! Nay, not fair that those pricks get all the fun – with their big raucous voices and one dozen weekly fucks . . . cave mouths, shout, burp and Guinness soaked . . . If I dare do that . . . 'What an old scrubber-slag-head' utter their fast and vicious lips . . . so I'd like to be a fella. Strolling down the front with the lads and making minute and limited wars with knife-worn splatter and invective splurge. And not have the emblem of his scummy lust to Persil out with hectic scrub . . . just my Johnny tool to keep from harm and out of mischief . . . my snarling beasty to water and feed from time to time to rotten time . . . to dip my wick into any old dark and hot with no conscience or love groan . . .

Oh let me be a bloke and sit back curseless, nor forever join the queue of curlered birds outside the loo for dire-emergency . . . do we piss more than men or something . . . nor break my heels in escalators and flash my ass, ascending stairs, to the vile multitude who fantasize me in their quick sex-lustered movies in which I am cast as the queen of slut and yield . . . let me be a bloke and wear trousers stuffed and have pectorals instead of boobs, abdominal and latissimus-dorsi, a web of knotted muscular armature to whip my angered fist into the flesh-pain of sprach-offenders who dare to cast on me their leery cautious minces . . . stab them with fear and have a dozen flesh-hot weekly . . . sleep well and mum fussed, breakfast shoved, 'who's been a naughty boy then', to this pastry wreck of skin and bone gasping in his bed skyving work through riotous folly, bloodlet assault and all night bang and 'our lad's a lad, and sown his wild then has he and did you cut yourself a slice' . . . while 'get yourself to the office Sylv or you'll be late,' and the sack in its bed is parlering for another cup of rosy. He's lying in bed whiles I'm on the Underground getting goosed in the rush hour between Mile End and Tottenham Court Road by some creepy asshole with dandruff, a wife and three accidental kids and who's probably in the accounts department . . . most perverts come from there.

* eye up

Ivanov

Anton Chekhov

Penguin, London 1973

Act 2 Scene 3

SASHA:

Oh, that's all nonsense. Nonsense! No one bought cows or infected them, it was all Borkin's idea that he went round boasting about. When Ivanov heard of it he had Borkin going round for a couple of weeks apologizing. Ivanov's only fault is being weak and not having enough go in him to chuck out friend Borkin, and he's wrong to trust people too much. He's been robbed and fleeced left, right and centre – anyone who liked has made a packet out of Ivanov's idealistic plans.

Why must they talk such nonsense? Oh, how boring, boring, boring. Ivanov, Ivanov, Ivanov – is there nothing else to talk about? [*Goes towards the door and returns.*] I'm surprised. [*To the young men.*] I'm really surprised how long-suffering you all are. Don't you ever get tired of sitting round like this? The very air's stiff with boredom. Can't you say something, amuse the girls or move around a bit? All right, if you've nothing to talk about but Ivanov, then laugh or sing or dance or something.

Would you mind listening for a moment? If you don't want to dance or laugh or sing, if you're bored with that, then please, please, just for once in your lives, if only for the novelty or surprise or fun of the thing – join forces and think up something brilliantly witty between you. Let it be rude or vulgar if you like, but funny and original. Or else do some small thing together which may not add up to all that much, but does at least look vaguely enterprising and might make the girls sit up and take notice for once in their lives. Look, you all want to be liked, don't you? Then why not try to be likeable? There's something wrong with you all, and no mistake. The sight of you's enough to kill the flies or start the lamps smoking. Yes, there's something wrong – I've told you thousands of times and I'll go on telling you – something wrong with you all, wrong, wrong, wrong!

Act 3 Scene 4

SASHA:

That's right – it's just what you need. Break something, smash things or start shouting. You're angry with me and it was silly of me to come here. All right, let off steam then, shout at me, stamp your feet. Come on, work up a rage. [*Pause.*] Come on then . . .

There's a great deal men don't understand. Any girl prefers a failure to a success because we're all fascinated by the idea of love in action. Action love, don't you see? Men are busy with their work, and love's very much in the background for them. You talk to your wife, stroll round the garden with her, pass the time of day nicely and have a little cry on her grave – and that's that. But love is our whole existence! I love you, and that means

I long to cure your unhappiness and go with you to the ends of the earth. If you go up in the world, I'll be with you, and if you fall by the wayside, I'll fall too. For instance, I'd love to spend all night copying your papers or watching to see that no one woke you up. Or I'd walk a hundred miles with you. I remember once about three years ago, at threshing time. You came to see us covered with dust, sunburnt, tired out – and asked for a drink. By the time I brought you a glass, you were lying on the sofa, dead to the world. You slept about twelve hours in our house and I stood guard at the door all the time to stop anyone going in. And I felt so marvellous. The more effort you put into love, the better it is – I mean the more strongly it's felt, do you see? . . .

It's time I went. Good-bye. I'm afraid our honest doctor might feel in duty bound to report my presence to Anna. Now listen. Go straight to your wife and stay with her, just stay put. If you have to stay a year, stay a year. If it has to be ten years, make it ten. Do your duty. Grieve for her, beg her forgiveness, weep – all as it should be. And above all, don't neglect your affairs.

Well, may God preserve you. You can forget me completely. Just drop me a line every couple of weeks, and I'll think I'm lucky to get that. And I'll be writing to you.

Ourselves Alone

Anne Devlin

Faber & Faber, London 1986

Act 2 Scene 1

DONNA:

The devil's back. He was lying with his head on my pillow this morning. When I woke up I recognized him immediately. Even though it's been years. [*Pause.*] The first time I ever saw him, he was standing in the corner of the room. I could feel something watching me. I had the bedclothes tucked up almost to my nose, so that I had to peer carefully round the room - and there he was. He seemed to grow out of the corner until he was towering over me. I panicked because I felt I was suffocating. My first husband was with me at the time. He called a doctor. He said I had asthma. The funny thing was, I really didn't get over my asthma attacks until my husband was interned. And I haven't seen the devil since. [*Pause.*] Until this morning. Liam bent over and kissed me goodbye as he was leaving. The trouble was he blocked my mouth and I couldn't breathe through my nose so I kept having to break away from him. When he'd gone, I closed my eyes and tried to get some sleep before the child woke. That was when I heard the door open. I thought Liam had come back so I opened my eyes, and there he was, the devil. If he had any hair at all it was red. He climbed on top of the bed and put his head on the pillow next to me. I felt so sick at the sight of him because I knew I didn't have the strength to struggle any more. I said: 'Please leave me alone.' I was very surprised when he replied. He's never spoken to me before. He said very quietly, 'All right, Donna.' And do you know - he vanished. But I don't believe he's really gone. He never really goes away.

Statements After an Arrest Under the Immorality Act

Athol Fugard

Oxford University Press, London 1974

WOMAN:

I don't understand . . . You can't. Don't even try. [*Carefully examines one of his shoes.*] Dust on his shoes. Him. His feet. His thoughts. A man . . . walking, from Bontrug to here, the town, to me . . . and then back again. [*Pause.*] One night I watched him through the window, walk away, quietly, quickly, and disappear down the street. I tried to imagine . . . [*Pause.*] I can't. [*Very carefully replaces the shoe as she found it. His clothes. She is trying hard to understand.*] There is no water in Bontrug! . . . I'm not thirsty . . . I don't understand . . . He uses the back door. He can't come to me any other way. When I heard the knock and opened it, the first time, wondering who it was . . . and saw him . . . No! I didn't. I saw a coloured man . . . I was not surprised. Because it was the back door.

I didn't have any of the books he mentioned . . . but I knew what he wanted and I found something else that I thought would help him. I said if there was anything I could do to help he must just tell me.

He always used my office. It started to seem so silly. Nobody was reading the books he needed. Only a few people ever went to that side of the library.

I found myself seeing books and articles in newspapers which I thought would help him. He's a very fast reader . . . and shy . . . at first . . . but once we started talking it was almost hard to keep up with him. And exciting. For me too. Even going home after I'd closed the library began to be different. I had something to do, and think about at night. You see, the library is not very busy . . . there's not all that much to look after.

I . . . I put off the light . . .

I stood there . . . I knew why I had put off the light . . . But once I had put it off . . . I was . . . hesitant . . . I was nervous . . . I wasn't sure what to do next . . . Well . . . he . . . he didn't move or do or say anything . . . I knew it was so hard for him that if I didn't do something . . . nothing would happen . . . so I . . .

[*Pause.*]

I knew where he was . . . So I took a few . . . paces . . . towards him . . . My hand came in contact with his . . . coat or jacket . . . There was another moment of hesitation . . . I had found him. And then . . .

[*Pause.*]

I moved in close to him. I knew that the response coming from him was the same. I wouldn't have had the courage if I didn't know what he felt . . . that he . . . So I leant against him . . . his shoulder . . .

[*Pause.*]

He put his arms around me . . . It felt like he . . . there was . . . his lips . . . yes. Then his lips touched the top of my head . . . it's very hard to remember anything.

[*Pause.*]

I know that we finally did kiss each other. Please, do I have to . . . please, it's very hard for me.

[*Pause.*]

So . . . so then . . . yes . . . So then we made love . . .

I switched off the light. Yes. Yes. Guilty. No doubt about it. Guilty of taking my chance and finding him. Hands, eyes, ears, nose, tongue . . . totally guilty. Nothing is innocent.

Camille

Pam Gems

From *Three Plays*,
Penguin Plays, 1985

Act 1

MARGUERITE:

You want to know? You want to know? What do you know? I know the way you live! Hot-house grapes, lofts full of apples, figs with bloom on them . . . stables, libraries, a fire in your room. [*She lopes, fiery and restless*] I used to clean the grates with my mother . . . five o'clock in the morning on tiptoe while you all snored. I saw them! The rugs, the pictures, the furniture . . . chandeliers . . . music room, ballrooms . . . all a hundred metres from where we lived on potatoes and turnips, and slept, the seven of us together, in a coach-house loft.

[*Pause*]

At thirteen, I became a housemaid. I slept in an attic . . . my own bed, you can't believe the bliss! I couldn't wait to get up in the morning! To be in such a palace . . .

After two years *Monsieur le Marquis* took me into his bed. It was his habit with the younger maids. It kept him young. A year later I had our son. . . .

You have no idea what difference a child makes. Your life is quite changed. For ever. Of course, with a man, this can never happen. Not in the same way. . . .

You're no longer alone. You're connected . . .

Whether you wish it or not . . . whether you see the child or not. It's there, part of you.

[*Pause*]

[*Light*] I hardly ever see him. He thinks I'm his aunt.

[*She pauses*]

I was dismissed, of course. I went to my mother's sister and sat by the river wondering what to do. I had no money. The most sensible thing seemed to be to drown myself.

[*Pause*]

And then, one morning . . . my cousin came into my room. I was putting on my stockings – he started to shake. I didn't have the strength to push him away. Afterwards, he put his finger to his lips, and gave me a gold coin.

And there it was. I knew. All of a sudden. How to do it. How to go through the magic door. How to be warm, how to be comfortable . . . eat fine food, wear fine clothes, read fine books, listen to fine music. I had the key. A golden key.

The Madwoman of Chaillot

Jean Giraudoux

Translated by Maurice Valency

Hill and Wang, New York 1958

Act 1

THE RAGPICKER:

The world has changed . . .

. . . people are not the same. The people are different. There's been an invasion. An infiltration. From another planet. The world is not beautiful any more. It's not happy . . .

. . . there was a time when you could walk around Paris, and all the people you met were just like yourself. A little cleaner, maybe, or dirtier, perhaps, or angry, or smiling – but you knew them. They were you. Well, Countess, twenty years ago, one day, on the street, I saw a face in the crowd. A face, you might say, without a face. The eyes – empty. The expression – not human. Not a human face. It saw me staring, and when it looked back at me with its gelatine eyes, I shuddered. Because I knew that to make room for this one, one of us must have left the earth. A while after, I saw another. And another. And since then, I've seen hundreds come in – yes – thousands.

You've seen them yourself. Their clothes don't wrinkle. Their hats don't come off. When they talk, they don't look at you. They don't perspire.

They buy the models out of shop windows, furs and all. They animate them by a secret process. Then they marry them. Naturally, they don't have children.

They don't do any work. Whenever they meet, they whisper, and then they pass each other thousand-franc notes. You see them standing on the corner by the Stock Exchange. You see them at auctions – in the back. They never raise a finger – they just stand there. In theater lobbies, by the box office – they never go inside. They don't do anything, but wherever you see them, things are not the same. I remember well the time when a cabbage could sell itself just by being a cabbage. Nowadays it's no good being a cabbage – unless you have an agent and pay him a commission. Nothing is free any more to sell itself or give itself away. These days, every cabbage has its pimp.

Little by little, the pimps have taken over the world. They don't do anything, they don't make anything – they just stand there and take their cut. It makes a difference. Look at the shopkeepers. Do you ever see one smiling at a customer any more? Certainly not. Their smiles are strictly for the pimps. The butcher has to smile at the meat-pimp, the florist at the rose-pimp, the grocer at the fresh-fruit-and-vegetable-pimp. It's all organized down to the slightest detail . . .

So now you know why the world is no longer happy. We are the last of the free people of the earth. You saw them looking us over today. Tomorrow, the street singer will start paying the song-pimp, and the garbabe-pimp will be after me. I tell you, we're finished. It's the end of free enterprise in this world!

Les Liasons Dangereuses

Christopher Hampton

Faber & Faber, London 1985

MERTEUIL:

I had no choice, did I, I'm a woman. Women are obliged to be far more skilful than men, because who ever wastes time cultivating inessential skills?

I had to invent not only myself, but ways of escape no one else has ever thought of, not even I, because I had to be fast enough on my feet to know how to improvise. And I've succeeded, because I always knew I was born to dominate your sex and avenge my own.

When I came out into society, I was 15, I was Cécile's age, I'd already realized that the role I was condemned to, namely to keep quiet and do as I was told, gave me the perfect oppportunity to listen and pay attention: not to what people told me, which was naturally of no interest, but to whatever it was they were trying to hide. I practised detachment. I learned how to look cheerful when I was angry and how to smile pleasantly while, under the table, I stuck a fork into the back of my hand. I became not merely impenetrable, but a virtuoso of deceit. Needless to say, at that stage nobody told me anything: and it wasn't pleasure I was after, it was knowledge. But when, in the interests of furthering that knowledge, I told my confessor I'd done 'everything', his reaction was so appalled, I began to get a sense of how extreme pleasure might be. No sooner had I made this discovery than my mother announced my marriage: so I was able to contain my curiosity and arrived in Monsieur de Merteuil's arms a virgin . . . He gave me little cause for complaint: and the minute I began to find him something of a nuisance, he very tactfully died.

I used my year of mourning to complete my studies: I consulted the strictest moralists to learn how to appear; philososphers to find out what to think; and novelists to see what I could get away with.

A few simple principles. Only flirt with those you intend to refuse: then you acquire a reputation for invincibility, whilst slipping safely away with the lover of your choice. Never write letters. Get them to write letters. Aways be sure they think they're the only one. Win or die.

Total Eclipse

Christopher Hampton

Faber & Faber, London 1969

ISABELLE:

One night, I was woken up by a terrible crash from his room. I rushed up there and found my brother lying face down on the floor, naked. He told me he had opened his eyes and it was dawn, and time to go, to lead his caravan of ivory and musk to the coast. It was time to leave, and he had leapt out of bed . . . After that, he refused to take any drugs again for a long time. He used to spend whole days crying.

It was a very bad summer - there was rain and fog, and the crops were ruined by frost. He kept saying that he wanted to go back to the sun, and that the sun would heal him, and eventually he left for Marseilles and I went with him. He intended to travel on from there to Aden, but when we got there he was too ill, and he went back into hospital.

It was only when he was dying that I realized he was a poet. When he was delirious, he spoke so gently and beautifully, that even the doctors came to listen. Often what he said made no sense, it was confused and strange, and sometimes he spoke in Arabic, but at the time it seemed perfectly easy to understand. He was in a coma for most of the last week, but on the day before he died he revived a little, and dictated a letter to a steamship company, booking a passage to Aden. He wanted the sun so much . . .

It's getting dark. I must go.

The Bay at Nice

David Hare

Faber & Faber, London 1986

SOPHIA:

I think less and less of love. What does love have to do with it? What matters is not love, but what the other person makes you. When I stand next to Grigor, it's clear, he is a dutiful man. He's a model servant of the State. Next to him, I look only like a fortunate woman who must struggle every day to deserve the luck she's had in marrying someone so worthwhile. That is my role. In marriages everyone gets cast. The strong one, the weak. The quick one, the slow. The steady, the giddy. It's set. Almost from the moment you meet. You don't notice it, you take it for granted, you think you're just *you*. Fixed, unchangeable. But you're not. You're what you've been cast as with the other person. And it's all got nothing to do with who you really are.

With Grigor, I'm dowdy, I'm scatterbrained, I'm trying to prove myself. All the standards are his. Grigor, of course, has nothing to prove. He's a headmaster at thirty-seven, the Party approves of him. He can always find his shirts in the drawer. I usually can. But Usually is no good next to Always. 'Usually' becomes a great effort of will. All I can do . . . no, all I can *be* is an inadequate, minor commentary on Grigor's far more finished character. Grigor and Sophia. After ten years we each have our part. Whereas when I'm with . . . this other man . . . then suddenly I'm quite someone else.

Plenty

David Hare

Faber & Faber, London 1984

Scene 4

SUSAN:

I want to move on. I do desperately want to feel I'm moving on.

I work so hard I have no time to think. The office is worse. Those brown invoices go back and forth, import, export . . .

They get heavier and heavier as the day goes on, I can barely stagger across the room for the weight of a single piece of paper, by the end of the day if you dropped one on the floor, you would smash your foot. The silence is worse. Dust gathering. Water lapping beyond the wall. It seems unreal. You can't believe that because of the work you do ships pass and sail across the world. [*She stares a moment.*] Mr Medlicott has moved into my office.

Or rather, more sinister still he has removed the frosted glass between our two offices.

I came in one morning and found the partition had gone. I interpret it as the first step in a mating dance. I believe Medlicott stayed behind one night, set his ledger aside, ripped off his tweed suit and his high collar, stripped naked, took up an axe, swung it at the partition, dropped to the floor, rolled over in the broken glass till he bled, till his whole body streamed blood, then he cleared up, slipped home, came back next morning and waited to see if anything would be said. But I have said nothing. And neither has he. He puts his head down and does not lift it till lunch. I have to look across at his few strands of hair, like seaweed across his skull. And I am frightened of what the next step will be.

The sexual pressure is becoming intolerable.

One day there was a condom in his turn-up. Used or unused I couldn't say. But planted without a doubt. Again, nothing said. I tried to laugh it off to myself, pretended he'd been off with some whore in Limehouse and not bothered to take his trousers off, so that after the event the condom had just absent-mindedly fallen from its place and lodged alongside all the bus tickets and the tobacco and the Smarties and the paper-clips and all the rest of it. But I know the truth. It was step two. And the dance has barely begun.

The Secret Rapture

David Hare

Faber & Faber, London 1989

ISOBEL:

I'm not myself. I'm being turned into a person whose only function is to suffer. And believe me, it bores me just as much as it bores you.

Oh God, I can't explain. Don't you understand? It's why I never talk to you. It's why I never look at you. I can't find a way of describing what's happened, without seeming to be disgustingly cruel. There we are, you see, now I look at you, you're flinching already . . .

And I'm standing here thinking, this is just stupid, I'm no longer in love with you. Why don't I just give you the push?

Why don't I just tell you to leave? As any sensible girl would. Why? Because, actually, there's a good part of me which is very fond of you. And wants to work with you. And hold on to what is best in you. So the fact is, I find it very hard.

I know you love me. God knows, you say it often enough.

I don't say that to be cruel. But I never hear the words without sensing something's being asked of me. The words drain me. From your lips they've become a kind of blackmail. They mean, I love you and *so* . . . *So* I am entitled to be endlessly comforted and supported and cheered . . . [*She smiles.*] Oh, yes, and I've been happy to do it. I comforted. I supported. I cheered. Because I got something back. But it's gone. [*She shrugs slightly.*] We both know it. Yet you want some period in which we both flounder together. Hang on tight while we get sad. But I don't want to be sad. No one can remember now, but the big joke is, by temperament I'm actually an extremely cheerful girl. That's what's so silly. I'm strong. You sap my strength. Because you make me feel guilty. I can never love you as much as you need. Now I see that. So I've done a great deal of suffering. But that's over. I'm ready to move on.

KATHERINE:

Please don't leave me. Please, Isobel. Just stay for tonight. I don't know what to do. It's all such an effort. Like at school one term I worked really hard. I came fifteenth. I thought, this is stupid. Other people come second without trying. Why has God made me so fucking mediocre? The first boyfriend I had, it was the same. I adored him. I gave myself over. I couldn't get enough of him. Then one day he just stopped sleeping with me. Bang. Just like that. No warning. It happened again, the next three boyfriends I had. I thought, oh I see, there is something about me which is actually repulsive. After a while men don't want me. [*She thinks a moment.*] Well, that feeling is hard. [ISOBEL *just listens, smoking her cigarette, not reacting.*] That night in the restaurant, I knew I couldn't do it. I just looked at them. I could see what they were thinking. She is not confident. I do not want to do business with her. They said, 'Oh, of course, you can't have a drink, can you?' It made me so angry. I thought, count to five. It's like they have to say it. Just to make you feel worse. So they all start drinking vodka. In these really posh surroundings. They keep drinking more. And I think, oh God, you as well. Please give me a break. Just look at me as if you trust me. as if there were a little goodness in me. Then they say, 'Well, of course, you never really thought we'd give you the contract, did you? This can hardly come as a surprise.' [*She smiles.*] What do you do? I just want to hurt them. The managing director is eating a little bird. He keeps picking little bits out of his teeth. And drinking more vodka. And laughing. He says, 'No hard feelings.' I start counting to five. I don't even get to three. I suddenly yell out, 'Yes, there fucking well are. There *are* hard feelings. Because you have all the power. And you love to exercise it. And oil it with vodka. And smile your stupid shiny smiles. And you have just ditched me, you have just landed me, right back, right back into my terrible unconfidence . . .' [*She shakes her head.*] You know what happened. I reached for a drink. A few minutes later I picked up my knife. [*She shrugs slightly and turns to* ISOBEL.] It wasn't *so* wrong. Was it? At least I was alive. Not like now.

Wrecked Eggs

David Hare Faber & Faber, London 1986

GRACE:

No. I feel helpless. Don't you ever feel helpless? Like, at the moment my life is in real estate. I'm working for a developer. He's one of the most powerful men in New York. Tiny office, dark suits, forty. His wife, his oldest son, and his secretary. That's his whole staff. And from his two-room office, he's trying to tear down twelve blocks on the West Side of New York. [*She sweeps with her arm.*] Docks are going to go. And houses. There's a park. There are shops. There are old apartment buildings. What we call *life*, in fact, that's what he's planning to remove. And in its place . . . you can imagine . . . you've seen it before he's even built it, it's dark, it's brutal, it's brown. It's eighty storeys of air-conditioned nothing. Great subdivided sections of air full of profit. For no conceivable human purpose at all.

[ROBBIE *is about to interrupt, but* GRACE *anticipates.*]

All right, that's it, that's OK, let's say it's not even to be argued with. It's progress. He comes to *me*. He says, of course I hate personal publicity. I say, who doesn't? It's a given. It's why film stars ride in thirty-foot black limos – to be inconspicuous. It's why they have loud voices in restaurants, and employ people like me. Because they hate publicity so much. 'What do you want,' I said, 'a new image? People to like you? A positive slant on all this?' Oh no,' he said 'I just need a black fireball of controversy. That way things will just burn themselves out.' [*She leans forward.*] And he's *clever*, you see. He's not frightened. He understands the process. We go for the cover of a New York magazine. 'The loathsome face of a property developer!' And inside it says 'But he gives money to charity.' So he's what magazines call 'complex'. He's got two sides to him. Well! He attends his children's school play. And people eat this crap, they love it, it's called personality. He's an asshole, *but.* What is he like? What is he like? is the only question. The question is never 'Is this right or wrong?' [*She shakes her head, suddenly vehement.*] It's not 'Shall we do this?' 'Should this be done?' No, it's 'Do we like the guy who's doing this? Is he a nice guy?' Not even nice, is he good copy? Then, hell, let him do what he wants. He wants a concentration camp for millionaires on the West Side? Let him have it. He's an interesting person. Forget the people who live on those blocks right now. They have no personality. They'll never make the cover. So they must be moved out of the way.

Yes and After

Michael Hastings

Penguin, London 1962

Scene 2

CAIRY:

It hit the barrier. And – and you were dead. One minute you are looking at – it comes charging towards you, hits you, and you don't see any more. You haven't got any eyes. Or heart. That clock downstairs – it's beating like a heart. I can hear it quite plain. That's what tells our time – our hearts – ticking away.

[*Joking.*] My heart's on my wrist! . . . you were dead. The car had twisted over, and rammed your head against the wall . . .

You remember the Whip at the fair? When the car swung round and lost a wheel, the carriage shot through the barrier at an old man and a boy – your age. The old man started to run but it caught you and rammed your head against the wall. You saw it. I needn't tell you! And that clanging the ambulance made! You did see it. Yes. I was with you. And the most beautiful moment. You said it. That it was the loveliest second in your life. We were up there, right on the top of the switchback! You couldn't be any higher. In the back of the car. As it dipped, and we stood up for a moment. There was everything beneath us. Nothing was missed out. The lights, and far out to the end of London. You could see it stop. There were cows, and streets, and tall buildings and things, then a park and gas-works. Quiet sort of colour, and the roads were less sharp. Didn't we stand up and shout out! What did you say after that ? . . . You only learn to love something by seeing enough of it. We saw enough! We saw so much then, there were millions of people, you were in love with the whole world. Go on – listen Terry – I saw it then more than ever before. I'd never been up in a plane. When I looked at all that ground. People I had never spoken to, millions, they'd never heard of me. I couldn't shout loud enough, up there, to tell even one of them who I was. And that I loved them! I'm so small . . . If they could hear my name, once. I did once; I wrote to the personal column in an evening paper; I was willing to pay double – I told them. All I wanted was a simple line – like 'I'm Henry Johnson'. But they refused! They said it didn't mean anything! It wasn't a trick-advertisement, or a message home, it didn't do anybody any good. That was the worst thing to say. It would have helped me. Wouldn't it? . . . Does everything in this world have to be of use to somebody, can't the smallest thing just stand there, and people take notice of it, just because it is being there?

Low Level Panic

Clare McIntyre

Nick Hern Books, London 1989

Scene 1

JO:

If I could grow six inches and be as fat as I am now I'd be really tall and thin. I could stretch out all the fat on my legs till they were long and slender and I'd go to swanky bars and smoke menthol cigarettes and I'd wrap my new legs round cocktail stools and I'd smooth myself all over with my delicate hands and I'd have my hair up so you could see my neck. I'd save all the pennies I see lying about on the streets in an old whisky bottle then I'd go out and buy silky underwear with lots of lace on it and suspenders and that's what I'd wear. I wouldn't wear anything else because that would spoil it. I'd wear that and a lot of make-up and I'd snake my way around bars and hotels in Mayfair and I'd be able to drink whatever I like. I'd have cocktails and white wine out of bottles with special dates on them in tall glasses that were all dewy with cold and I'd smile a lot. I wouldn't laugh. I wouldn't guffaw. I'd just smile and show my teeth and I'd really be somebody then.

I'd have a fur. As soon as I got inside I'd take it off.

They'd see me approach. Just my feet in 'fuck me' stilettos and the door would open like magic and uniformed men would be bowing. They wouldn't look at me: their eyes would be averted. I'd be able to get through doors without even turning the handles.

I wouldn't need anything, I wouldn't even have a bag. I'd have my lipstick on a chain round my neck. I'd play with my drink a bit, wiping the dewy bits off the glass and feeling my way up and down the stem with my fingers. Then I'd go to the loo and do my lipstick.

Then, I'd meet someone.

We wouldn't talk. Christ. We'd be really . . . We'd just *be* there.

We'd just drink: play with our drinks and look at each other. We wouldn't really drink them. We wouldn't get pissed. We'd sit while the ice melted in them and they got all watery and we'd look at each other. He'd look at me that is. I'd know he was looking at me and I'd look at myself in the mirror behind the bar. The whole place would be mirrors and he'd be looking at my legs . . . Then we'd leave. People would crash their cars when I got out in the street. There'd be cars jumping over each other to pick me up, men running towards me, desperate to get a closer look and try and touch me, touch my fur. But I wouldn't give anything away. I wouldn't get involved. I'd be wearing sunglasses, enormous, dark ones so they wouldn't see into me. I'd just be an amazing pair of legs, in sunglasses getting into a car.

A great big American limousine.

Big enough for eight people across the back seat.

We'd go to his place.

I'd be an astonishingly beautiful, mysterious, fascinating woman. The kind of woman men dream about but hardly ever see. I wouldn't need to talk.

I could be dumb. I could be a mute. He might like that.

We'd be a beautiful couple.

But rich.

And glamorous. . . .

He might have a yacht. I could lounge about and go swimming. I'd dive in off the side of the boat. I'd be really good. I wouldn't have to hold my nose or hang on to the side. I'd go right under with my eyes open, do somersaults and all sorts just to get cool, go right down, dive down a long way and then float back up looking at the bright, bright blue above and my air bubbles bursting on the surface.

I'd climb back on to the boat, dry off, have a Campari and a smoke and listen to the music wafting up from below deck out into the open sunshine.

Christ it would be amazing. Christ. Think of it. All that blue and sea.

He might have a sense of humour. There's a chance. We might grow to like each other after a while.

We'd be a glamorous couple with a lot of money and a yacht. I wouldn't mind fucking that.

It'd be phenomenal. I'd feel brilliant about myself. I'd get really thin and I'd get tanned all over, even my armpits. That would be my sole occupation, getting tanned without any strap-marks. I'd love every single minute of it.

I'd fancy him to death.

Fucking makes the world go round. It's the only thing that makes being grown-up worthwhile.

Scene 2

MARY:

Maybe if I'd been wearing trousers it wouldn't have happened. I was only wearing a skirt because I'd just come from work and it's the kind of place where they like you to wear a skirt, that or smart trousers. Well, I haven't got any smart trousers so I have to wear a skirt. You're better off on a bike in trousers I know. It's obvious. But it's not as if I was going on a marathon. It takes ten minutes to cycle home at the outside. More like five. If that. I'm not really comfortable on a bike in a skirt: it just makes people look at your legs. But who's around at that time of night to look? Anyway I wasn't even on the bike: I was *going* to get on it. I was going to. It's not as if I was cycling along with my skirt up round my ears. I wasn't. I don't do silly things like that. I could have been getting into a car in a skirt. Would that have made a difference? I could have cycled to work wearing a pair of jeans and had my skirt folded up in one of the panniers but then it would have been all squashed and that wouldn't have gone down well at all with the management. Or I could have come to work on the bicycle wearing a skirt and could have changed into trousers to go home given that you're meant to be alright in the daylight but you're not safe at night. Or I could have walked to work and got a taxi home and I could have worn whatever I liked. But I'd still have been there, on the edge of the road at midnight, about to get on my bicycle or into a car or just been stuck there waiting for a taxi whether I'd been in a skirt or not, whether I had good legs or not, whether I was fifteen or menopausal or lame, I'd still have been there.

Scene 4

JO:

I sometimes wish I could tell someone that sometimes I just come home, go upstairs and masturbate. I might roam around the kitchen a bit first, pick at a couple of things; I have a look in the fridge. Sometimes I'll find myself checking out the house. I'll be in someone else's room for no reason at all, 'cept I suppose to see they're not there: looking for signs. I'm not nosey really. I'd never read anyone's letters.

I like to go upstairs and take all my clothes off and get under the bedcovers. I close the curtains but not completely. I like to see the daylight creep through. I lie there and think about what my body is like and about being somewhere else: somewhere hot and abroad. But my body feels soft and cool. I'm not sweaty at all. I'm quite, quite clean and perfumed.

I think about hitching in a flowery skirt and a very sexy top and wedge canvas shoes that have ties round the ankles. I always imagine my body a different shape to the way it is. I'm always very thin and light and what I think people think is the most desirable thing possible.

I always get picked up by two men in a lorry. I've tried imagining other things like military uniforms and all that but I don't get so whooped up about it. No, I get in this lorry and it's quite clear what the atmosphere is straight away. Then I'll do something provocative like shut my eyes and be half asleep and the bloke who isn't driving starts making love to me and it's all incredibly fast in my imagination and we get into the back bit of the lorry where they sleep at night and we make love as if we adore each other.

There's never a moment of worry. The men are never mean or anything. They both just want to make love to me. It's all very serious and passionate. I think they are very male. I don't really know what that means but. . . . The one who's driving must stop driving because then he is there as well and then it gets muddled because I think I've really had enough but I like to think of him watching us.

Then that's it. It never ends. There's no conclusion. We don't introduce each other and drive on. I mean I've never worked out what happens then. I've never had to. It just ends and I start thinking about something else.

I try to think about something else but I usually feel upset. I always feel upset actually and I'll hang on to my pillow and wrap myself in the sheet and cry a bit. Then I'll get up and wash my face and think 'Thank God no one knows what I think.'

I don't feel guilty. No one knows what goes on inside your head anyway. I just feel sad about everything that I do not have.

But it's awful to think like that. Isn't it? I mean it's completely untrue for a start. I've never actually felt that in my life. I haven't often hitched rides from lorry drivers on my own but when I have I haven't felt like touching them. I haven't really felt anything at all other than scared and thankful that they weren't trying to do anything.

I can't imagine for the life of me what I thought I was doing when I was hitchhiking. I think now I must have been mad. I could have got myself killed.

Scene 6

MARY:

I was walking past a poster one day.

It was an absolutely huge poster.

It was like the size of one of those ones that's on the way out to the airport, you know, like, like for Concorde or something.

But it wasn't sort of long across it was long upright.

And it looked so weird 'cos it just sort of stood out of the skyline.

And I just stopped and looked at it. I suppose it was advertising something but I didn't really see that. I just saw what it was, what was in the picture.

And there was a gorilla in the picture and he was holding on to a woman in a bikini.

He had one hand through her legs and gripping on to a thigh and his other arm was right round her and clutching on to her ribs and he had one thumb which was sort of half pulling off her bikini top.

And I looked at the woman and she looked like she was just mucking about really, you know, she, you know, her arms were just sort of thrown up in the air and her body was all sort of shiny. It didn't look like it was wet. It just looked like it had years and years of suntan oil on it. She was hairless and shiny and silky, like she would, you know, tall and thin.

And I looked at her and then I looked at her face.

And she had absolutely no expression at all.

There was no expression on her face at all.

I couldn't detect any expression.

I couldn't see that she was looking like anything.

At all.

She just, she didn't, it wasn't, she wasn't scared, she wasn't aroused. She just didn't look like anything at all.

She didn't even look as if she was in a daze.

And then I looked . . .

Her body. She didn't in her body look like anything at all either.

She didn't look like she was trying to get away. She just looked like she was posing there and the gorilla was holding on to her.

And I just wanted to ask her what she felt. I really, really wanted to ask her what she felt.

So I got into the picture. I walked up to it and as I got close to it I realised it was one of those relief pictures.

I climbed up on the hoarding that was beneath it and I got my feet on her feet. And actually when I was close up to it it was absolutely huge. It was really big. I mean as I was standing up, you know, I got to about her kneecap.

So I climbed up on this picture and I was standing on her

knees and I could just use all the relief bits to get me right up. And as I got towards the top I had to hold on to the gorilla's hand and I was levering myself up and finally I was standing on her breast and hanging on to her neck and then I got one knee on one of her shoulders.

And as I got up there I was face to face with her and her eyes were absolutely huge and they were com . . . they weren't focused. I wasn't sc . . . scared because they weren't focused. They weren't looking at me. I don't, I don't think they were looking at anything at all.

And as I got up there her head gently fell back and her mouth opened.

So I pulled myself up on both of her shoulders and looked into her mouth. And I just screamed and screamed and I nearly just fell off the picture because inside there wasn't anything at all.

She was completely empty.

And all I could see was the gorilla's thumb stuck through her crotch and he was wiggling it.

And as I looked away her head came back upright and her eyelids closed and opened and they were exactly like a doll's when you tilt the head of a doll back the eyelids open and shut.

Well I got off and on to the ground as fast as I could.

In some ways I was, I felt a lot happier they hadn't used anyone real to make the picture.

Don Juan

Molière

Translated by Nick Enright

Currency, Sydney 1984

Scene 3

DONA ELVIRA:

Don Juan! Will you do me the courtesy of an acknowledgement? Dare I hope that at least you might turn your face this way?

I can see you were not expecting me. And indeed you are surprised but not in the way I was hoping. Your manner makes me accept what I refused to believe. I am amazed that I could be so simple or so faint-hearted as to doubt my own betrayal when every sign confirms it. Each day my just suspicions spoke in vain. I rejected all thoughts of your guilt, and entertained a thousand silly fantasies of your innocence. But this welcome no longer allows me any doubt, and the glance that greeted me tells me more than I wish to know. Still, I would be pleased to hear from your own lips the reason for your departure. Speak, Don Juan, I beg you, and let us see how you may vindicate yourself.

Why not swear to me that your feelings are constant, that you love me for ever with unparalleled passion, that nothing could tear you away from me but death? Why not tell me matters of life and death forced you to depart without a word to me? That you are obliged to remain here some time? That I should go home now with the assurance that you will follow just as soon as you may? That you burn with desire to be reunited with me? That separation from me brings suffering like that of a body parted from its own soul? That is how you should defend yourself, not stand silent as you do now.

Ah! Criminal, now I see you as you are. But is it my misfortune that I see you too late, when my discovery can lead me only to despair. But know that your crime will not go unpunished, and that the Heaven you mock now will avenge my betrayal.

Do not think I shall exhaust myself here with reproaches and accusations! No, my rage will not expend itself in empty words, but keep itself hot for vengeance. I tell you again, faithless man, Heaven will punish you for the outrage you do me. And if Heaven holds no fear for you, then remember the anger of a wronged woman and fear that.

Scene 6

DONA ELVIRA:

Do not be surprised, Don Juan, to see me at this hour, dressed like this. I have a pressing reason for this visit, and what I have to say to you cannot wait. I come here no longer full of the anger that possessed me and you see me entirely altered from my state this morning. This is no longer the Dona Elvira who cursed you, whose injured soul made threats of vengeance. Heaven has driven from my soul all my unworthy passion for you, all the shameful torment of a gross and earthly love. In my heart it has left only compassion, and a love detached from the senses, without thought for itself, concerned only for you.

It is this love that brings me here for your good, to show you the will of Heaven, and to try to draw you back from the precipice towards which you run. Yes, Don Juan, I know all the excesses of your life. And the very Heaven which has touched my heart and shown me my own waywardness, has inspired me to come and seek you here, and speak to you on its behalf. Its mercy is exhausted by your sins, and its teribile wrath is ready to strike you. It can be averted only by immediate repentance. You may have less than one day to save yourself from the greatest of all misfortunes. I no longer feel any attachment to you. Thanks to Heaven I am recovered from my delusion. I have decided to return to the convent, where I shall devote the rest of my life to expiation of my sin, and earn pardon for my blind, reckless passion by fasting and prayer. But even in the cloister, I should be grieved to think that someone I loved so dearly should die wretchedly as a sign of Heaven's just anger. And it will be an unbelievable joy to me if I can lead you to escape the dreadful fate that threatens you. For love of God, Don Juan, give me this sweet comfort as a last favour. Do not deny me your salvation, which I beg of you with tears. And if your own cause does not move you, then be moved by my prayers and spare me the pain of seeing you condemned to eternal torment.

I loved you with the greatest tenderness. Nothing in the world was so dear to me as you. I abandoned my vows for you. I did everything for you. The only recompense I ask is that you reform your life and prevent your downfall. Save yourself, I beg you, for love of yourself or love of me. Once more, Don Juan, I beg it of you, with tears. And if you are untouched by the tears of a woman you have loved, I conjure you by whatever can touch you.

Now that I have spoken I shall go. That is all I had to say.

The Bells of Hell

John Mortimer

Samuel French, London 1978

Act 1 Scene 1

MADGE:

I prayed every night to be delivered from the temptation of Gavin Faber.

I wanted him passionately. But I knew that even to speak to him would be a sin. I prayed to God I wouldn't be chosen to accompany him on the Deprived Children's Seaside Outing . . .

They were denied! I was chosen. There was a child there - a pale little girl. Well, none of them had ever seen the sea before - or heard it. She thought the waves advanced on her furiously, roaring like a lion. She ran in terror from them, screaming. As I held her trembling in my arms I saw in her eyes such a fierce and fearless joy - it was exactly how I felt when I first saw the bulge in front of Gavin's Jansens!

If I touched it I knew I was condemned to Hellfire. And yet I felt it was my destiny to touch it, sooner or later.

The children lit a fire of driftwood and we sat round in a circle. Gavin led the community singing: 'Underneath the Spreading Chestnut Tree'. He touched his nipples, his forehead. He spread out his arms like branches. I watched him grow under the black wool of his Jansens as he gazed at me. The wind blew a sandstorm against my bare legs and my teeth chattered with excitement. I swore not to go near him, but on the charabanc home I pushed away the sour-smelling children with their wet towels and claimed a seat beside him! He had trousers on then. Pale grey flannel bags.

It would be a sin, I whispered to him, if I were to touch you there . . .

He told me - it wouldn't be a sin at all: that it was perfectly natural and God would understand . . .

From that moment I began to lose interest.

Judging from the appearance of his fly buttons my sudden boredom communicated itself. 'Don't be frightened,' he said. 'There's no sort of sin about it. God doesn't care twopence about a little nooky, provided it's done with sincerity!'

Well, if God wasn't going to take an interest - why should I?

The Storm

Alexander Ostrovsky

Progress Publishers, Moscow 1979

Episode 7

KATERINA:

How I did love to go to church! Each time it was as if I entered paradise, and I was not aware of the people around me, or of the passage of time, or of the ending of the service. It might have been but a single moment. Mama used to say the whole congregation looked at me in wonder. Just think, Varya! On sunny days the light would stream down through the windows of the dome in a bright column, and smoke from the incense would form clouds in this column of light, and as if angels were flying and singing among these clouds. And then again, Varvara, I would get up at night, and in our house, too, lamps burned in front of the icons day and night, and I would kneel in a corner and pray until morning. Or I would go out into the garden early in the morning when the sun was just coming up and fall on my knees and weep and pray and not know myself what I was weeping and praying for. And there they would find me. I cannot think what I asked for in my prayers, for I was in need of nothing, I had all my heart could desire. And what dreams I had, Varvara, what dreams! Golden temples, and fairy-tale gardens, and invisible voices singing, and a fragrance as of cypress, and trees and hills like are painted on the holy images and not at all like in real life. And again as if I was flying, flying, way up in the air . . . I still have such dreams, but not very often and not the same.

[*After a pause.*] I am going to die soon.

I know I am going to die. Oh, Varvara, something evil is happening to me, some evil spell is upon me! Never before have I felt like this. It's unlike anything I've ever known. As if I was about to begin life all over again, or . . . or . . I don't know what . . .

Like as if I was standing on the edge of a precipice and

somebody was pushing me and I had nothing to cling to.

A terrible longing keeps coming over me and I cannot free myself of it. I try to think – my thoughts escape me; I try to pray – I cannot pray. I form words with my lips, but my mind is full of something else. Like as if the devil was whispering dreadful things in my ear. And sometimes I have visions that make me ashamed of myself. What is it, Varvara? Something is going to happen, something dreadful is surely going to happen. At night I cannot sleep, I fancy I hear a murmur, like as if somebody was whispering lovesome words to me, whispering sweetness, gentle as a dove. I don't dream about the hills and trees of paradise any more, Varvara; I dream of somebody holding me in his arms, tight, oh, tight! and leading me away, and me going with him – away . . . away . . .

Oh dear, I shouldn't be telling you this.

Episode 10

KATERINA:

[*Alone, with the key in her hand.*] What is she doing? What is she thinking of? Is she mad? Yes, mad, that's what she is! My ruin; here it is, in my own hand. I'll throw it away, throw it far away, into the river, so that nobody will ever find it. Ah, dear God, it burns my fingers like a live coal. [*After some consideration.*] That's how we women come to a bad end. Is it a pleasure, think you, being locked up like this? Naturally, all sorts of ideas come into your head. Then a chance of escape comes along; some women are only too glad to seize it, rush in without thinking. How is it possible, without thinking, without weighing the consequences? Ruin is but a step away! Weep, then, and suffer torment the rest of your life! Imprisonment will only seem the more bitter. [*Silence.*] It *is* bitter, never to be able to do anything you want, oh, how bitter! Who doesn't shed tears over it? And none weep so much as we women do. Take me, now: I live in misery day after day, without seeing a ray of light and never hoping to. The longer I live the worse it gets. And now I have this sin on my conscience. [*Becomes lost in thought.*] If it wasn't for my mother-in-law . . . she's the one who has crushed me. It's because of her I've come to hate this house; the very walls are hateful. [*Gazes pensively at the key.*] Throw it away? Aye, I must throw it away. How did it ever fall into my hands? Here is temptation. Here is my ruin. [*Becomes suddenly alert.*] Someone is coming! How my heart is beating! [*Thrusts the key into her pocket.*] Nobody. A false alarm. How terrified I was! And I hid the key away. Well, then, that is what I was meant to do. That is my fate. After all, what harm can come from seeing him just once, if only from a distance? Or from speaking to him just once? But I promised my husband. Well, he didn't want to help me. Perhaps I will never have such a chance again. Blame yourself, then; the chance came and you were afraid to take it. What am I saying? Why am I trying to deceive myself? I would gladly die just to see him once! Why am I pretending? Throw the key away? Never, not for anything in the world! It belongs to me now. Come what may, I shall see Boris! Oh, if only night would come quickly!

Act 3 Episode 2

KATERINA:

[*alone*] Nowhere. Nowhere to be found. What could he be doing now, poor darling? Only to say good-bye to him, only that, and then . . . then I'm even ready to die. Why have I done this to him? It hasn't eased my lot any. Why couldn't I have met my fate alone?

Alas, I've ruined myself and him too, brought dishonour on myself, eternal disgrace to him; yes, yes, dishonour on myself, eternal disgrace to him. [*Pause.*] Let me recall what he said to me, what tender words he spoke to me. What were they now? [*Takes her head in her hands.*] Ah, me, I can't remember. I've forgotten everything. It's the nights, the nights that are so terrible! Everyone goes to bed, and I go too; everyone sleeps, but I lie there like in my grave. How fearful the darkness is! I hear noises, and singing, like at a funeral; only so soft I can hardly catch the sound, and far, far away . . . When the morning light comes, what a relief! But I don't want to get up; the same people, the same talk, the same torture. Why do they look at me like that? Why did they stop? They used to kill ones like me in days gone by, they say. They would have taken me and thrown me in the Volga. And a good thing; I would have been glad. But nowadays they say 'If we kill you, your sin will be atoned for; no, you must go on living and suffering for your sin!' Oh, I *am* suffering! How much longer will it go on? Why should I live? What have I to live for? There is nothing I want, nothing that pleases me, not even the light of day. But death doesn't come. I cry out for it, and it doesn't come. Everything I see and hear only makes the pain here [*putting her hand on her heart*] worse. Perhaps I would find some joy in life if I lived with him. And why shouldn't I? It makes no difference now, I am already a lost soul. How I long for him! Dear God, how I long for him! If I cannot see you, love, at least hear me from the distance! Sweet wind, carry to him my sorrow and my longing! Blessed saints, how I long for him! [*Goes to the river-bank and cries out in a loud voice.*] My love! My life! My soul! How I love you! Oh, answer me! Answer me! [*She weeps.*]

Special Offer

Harold Pinter

From *Revue Sketches,*
Faber & Faber, London 1991

SECRETARY:

Yes, I was in the rest room at Swan and Edgars, having a little rest. Just sitting there, interfering with nobody, when this old crone suddenly came right up to me and sat beside me. You're on the staff of the B.B.C. she said, aren't you? I've got just the thing for you, she said, and put a little card into my hand. Do you know what was written on it? MEN FOR SALE! What on earth do you mean? I said. Men, she said, all sorts, shapes and sizes, for sale. What on earth can you *possibly mean*? I said. It's an international congress, she said, got up for the entertainment and relief of lady members of the civil service. You can hear some of the boys we've got speak through a microphone, especially for your pleasure, singing little folk tunes we're sure you've never heard before. Tea is on the house and every day we have the best pastries. For the cabaret at teatime the boys do a rare dance imported all the way from Buenos Aires, dressed in nothing but a pair of cricket pads. Every single one of them is tried and tested, very best quality, and at very reasonable rates. If you like one of them by any of his individual characteristics you can buy him, but for you not at retail price. As you work for the B.B.C. we'll be glad to make a special reduction. If you're at all dissatisfied you can send him back within seven days and have your money refunded. That's *very* kind of you, I said, but as a matter of fact I've just been on leave, I start work tomorrow and am perfectly refreshed. And I left her where she was. Men for Sale! What an extraordinary idea! I've never heard of anything so outrageous, have you? Look – here's the card.

[*Pause.*]

Do you think it's a joke . . . or serious?

Time and the Conways

J. B. Priestley

Penguin, London 1969

CAROL:

I haven't exactly decided what to do yet, there are so many things to do . . . I could, of course, go on the stage and I've often thought of it. But I shouldn't want to be on the stage all the time – and when I wasn't playing a part, I'd like to be painting pictures – just for myself, y'know – daubing like mad – with lots and lots and lots of the very brightest paint – tubes and tubes of vermilion and royal blue and emerald green and gamboge and cobalt and Chinese white. And then making all kinds of weird dresses for myself. And scarlet cloaks. And black crepe-de-chine gowns with orange dragons all over them. And cooking! Yes, doing sausages and gingerbread and pancakes. And sitting on the top of mountains and going down rivers in canoes. And making friends with all sorts of people. And I'd share a flat or a little house with Kay in London, and Alan would come to stay with us and smoke his pipe, and we'd talk about books and laugh at ridiculous people, and then go to foreign countries . . . I'd get it all in somehow. The point is – to live. Never mind about money and positions and husbands with titles and rubbish – I'm going to live.

Phaedra

Jean Racine

Translated by Robert Lowell — Faber & Faber, London 1961

PHAEDRA:

You monster! You understood me too well! Why do you hang there, speechless, petrified, polite! My mind whirls. What have I to hide? Phaedra in all her madness stands before you. I love you! Fool, I love you, I adore you! Do not imagine that my mind approved my first defection, Prince, or that I loved your youth light-heartedly, and fed my treason with cowardly compliance, till I lost my reason. I wished to hate you, but the gods corrupt us; though I never suffered their abrupt seductions, shattering advances, I too bear their sensual lightnings in my thigh. I too am dying. I have felt the heat that drove my mother through the fields of Crete, the bride of Minos, dying for the full magnetic April thunders of the bull. I struggled with my sickness, but I found no grace or magic to preserve my sound intelligence and honor from this lust, plowing my body with its horny thrust. At first I fled you, and when this fell short of safety, Prince, I exiled you from court. Alas, my violence to resist you made my face inhuman, hateful. I was afraid to kiss my husband lest I love his son. I made you fear me (this was easily done); you loathed me more, I ached for you no less. Misfortune magnified your loveliness. I grew so wrung and wasted, men mistook me for the Sibyl. If you could bear to look your eyes would tell you. Do you believe my passion is voluntary? That my obscene confession is some dark trick, some oily artifice? I came to beg you not to sacrifice my son, already uncertain of his life. Ridiculous, mad embassy, for a wife who loves her stepson! Prince, I only spoke about myself! Avenge yourself, invoke your father; a worse monster threatens you than any Theseus ever fought and slew.

Bodies

James Saunders

Amber Lane Press, London 1979

Act 1

HELEN:

After we got to the States I slept a lot; every spare minute. We must have seemed a rather dull couple, staying home evenings, polite but unresponsive to neighbours, watching TV, being nice to each other; I wondered whether they took us for a typical English couple. One afternoon a neighbour called in to borrow some shortening, to make a few cookies for the kiddies. I offered her a cup of tea, we sat drinking it. Suddenly she said: 'Is there anything wrong? Is there anything I can do?' Her eyes were full of concern. I wonder what she would have done if I'd told her: 'Well, you see, my husband fell in love with a great friend of mine and was having an affair with her, so I fell in love with the husband, since he was a great friend of my husband, and I was having an affair with him; but we couldn't stand that, so my friend's husband, that is my lover, left his wife, and I went off and lived with him for a while, leaving the other two to more or less live with each other as well; but this didn't work either, so I'm back with my husband and she's back with hers. Which sounds fine on the face of it, an interesting experiment in alternative living, except that on the way a few things got lost. I don't believe in love any more, for instance, or trust, or fidelity, or the sanctity of anything at all, or truth, or value, or, I'm afraid, meaning; meaning I don't believe in. I don't believe in the innocent concern in those wide blue Country-and-Western eyes, Mrs Levington, with your nice comfy hubby who calls you honey and your kiddies and your cookies. I don't believe the world you live in is any more solid than mine. You've just been lucky so far.' But I didn't say that. I simply, suddenly, cried. And cried. And cried . . . But then we found the therapy. And after a while, everything was fine.

Savoury Meringue

James Saunders

Amber Lane Press, London 1980

HESSIAN:

Think I ought to jump into the breach then? Pull the cat out of the fire? Turn disaster into triumph through sheer force of personality, talent and my indomitable will? Get up and make you cry shall I? Get you in stitches with my inimitable wit? Like my life story with it, sure why not. I'll throw in a song and dance while I'm at it, why not, then strip off in case your attention's flagging and a quick fuck with any gentleman in the front row. Why not? Except I'm not going to. Do it your bloody selves. Be thyself and thyself alone, that's my motto. Perseverance.

[*Pause.*]

Six years, six years I had him round my neck. His name was Albert Ross believe it or not, well it should have been. He got the moral blackmail off to a fine art. Pulled me down into the shit like a grand master. He was paranoid. He'd lost a foot. He was impotent. He got boils. He got dandruff till he was cured by going bald. He was a right mess he should've been put down only no-one ever had the heart. Look at me he said. Look at my background. Look at my upbringing. Look at my hangups. Look at my boils. I'm disgusting I know that. You can't live with me, no-one can live with me, and keep their dinner down. I'm a cruel filthy thoughtless disgusting tyke and I'll drag you under. Leave me, I'm not worth it, I'll get by till I go rotten enough to die. The bastard. Took him six years to drag me under and I don't think he was trying all that hard. The only promise he ever kept. He reduced me to a heap of quivering human debris and he never stopped apologising till I went into the nursing home. The end of a beautiful relationship. He couldn't visit me of course, it was too painful for him, knowing he'd put me there. I finally got home there was a note on the mantelpiece, where else. Written on toilet paper if you'll believe me. He couldn't live with what he'd done to me so he'd gone off with a mutual friend. Took his boot his whips his spurs the lot, never again. It's all completely untrue of course, needless to say. I'm a happily married woman, his name's Ted and we've got two lovely kiddies a boy and a girl, that's a lie too, I'm not married, I'm just an actress on a stage and I'm sick of it, I'm not really.

A Scent of Flowers ★

James Saunders

Penguin, London 1965

ZOE:

Do you know what's happened? . . . A most unusual thing; I am completely . . . and utterly . . . happy. . . . Suddenly, I'm not hungry, I'm not thirsty, I don't care what's to become of me . . . I don't desire you . . . You may even be asleep . . . I can just feel your arm touching the back of my fingers . . . But I don't have to raise my hand to stroke your skin . . . It's as though I'd found my way inside a little crystal ball . . . somewhere outside it's all still going on. People are hurting one another and crying out . . . Only just for a moment they've forgotten about me . . . I'm complete . . . I'm at rest . . . And afraid to move . . .

The Real Thing

Tom Stoppard

Faber & Faber, London 1983

DEBBIE:

House of Cards wasn't about anything, except did she have it off or didn't she? What a crisis. Infidelity among the architect class. Again.

As if having it off is infidelity.

Most people think *not* having it off is *fidelity*. They think all relationships hinge in the middle. Sex or no sex. What a fantastic range of possibilities. Like an on/off switch. Did she or didn't she. By Henry Ibsen. Why would you want to make it such a crisis?

It's what comes of making such a mystery of it. When I was twelve I was obsessed. Everything was sex. Latin was sex. The dictionary fell open at *meretrix*, a harlot. You could feel the mystery coming off the word like musk. *Meretrix*! This was none of your *mensa*-a-table, this was a flash from the forbidden planet, and it was everywhere. History was sex, French was sex, art was sex, the Bible, poetry, penfriends, games, music, everything was sex except biology which was obviously sex but obviously not *really* sex, not the one which was secret and ecstatic and wicked and a sacrament and all the things it was supposed to be but couldn't be at one and the same time – I got that in the boiler room and it turned out to be biology after all. That's what free love is free of – propaganda.

Sisters ★

David Storey

Penguin, London 1980

Act 1

CAROL:

You were such a dreamer, Aid . . . those schemes: those wonderful fantasies. Do you remember lying in bed at night: how I'd come into yours when it got very cold and you used to cuddle me and tell me stories?

Do you remember that night: the last Christmas when we hung up a sack for presents: *I* hung up a sack for presents – you were a little bit above it then – and you leaned across to my bed and woke me up? You said, 'Can you hear that, Carol?' And when I raised my head you said . . . 'Angels.' And from somewhere – it must have been the end of the road – came the sound of singing: a choir. It was the most angelic thing I'd ever heard. And since I was cold you took me into your bed: we lay together and listened. I believed . . . oh I believed for so long I was hearing angels. Christmas night had so much mystery then . . . that mysterious presence that delivered presents . . . that preoccupation with the sky and stars, with goodness and generosity and giving. And do you remember what you said, lying there? 'The one present I want I think I might have. Not tonight, another night.' And when I asked you what it was you said, 'I intend to go away. I'll become so famous that people will follow me in the street. Everyone will look: everyone will know my name. And everywhere I go I shall take you with me.' I felt so good; I felt so proud: I felt protected. It was as if it had happened already. You made it so real: the places we went to: the people who saw us: the cars we rode in. It was so extraordinary, Aid, that even now, each Christmas, I think of it. I look out at that sooty road, with all those identical houses, and think, 'One day . . . that really will happen.' Out there is a magic I glimpsed as a child. You *made* me a dreamer.

The Friends

Arnold Wesker

Penguin, London 1978

Act 1 Scene 1

ESTHER:

What is it? Why is everyone standing around? I know what it is. It's depression time again. I'm dying and you want me to make it easier for you by pretending I'm not, isn't it? Come on now, we're all too clever for dramatic deceits like that. And what's more, your silence and pretending make my misery worse. Much, much worse. MACEY! I want to go on living! ROLAND! I *don't* want to die. MANFRED,
SIMONE, TESSA! All of you. I-do-not-want-to-die. [*Pause.*] My God, that was cruel of me, wasn't it. Oh, forgive me, everyone, don't take notice. I didn't mean to give you pain.

Yes, I did. I did want to give pain. I should say I don't mind, make it easier for you, but I do – I do – I just do. [*Long pause.*]

Do you know anybody who was prepared to die? Despite all the suffering and the knowledge of suffering and man's inhumanity, everyone wants to go on living – for ever and ever, gloriously.

Some people of course know that when they're old they'll become tired and ready to go; or else they grow to despise themselves so much for not being what they thought they were that they become anxious and eager to fade out. Not me, though. Just not me. I can't tell you how much I cherish everything. I know there's a lot that's obscene and ugly but it's never been too oppressive, I've always had the capacity not to be oppressed. *You* know that, don't you, Roland? In the end there's such sweetness, such joy in hidden places. I want to stay on and not miss anything. I want to stay with you, all of you, close and warm and happy. Why shouldn't I want that? And think – all those things I haven't done. Every year the world finds something new to offer me: another man makes music or carves an impossible shape out of the rocks or sings us a poem.

Someone is always rising up, taking wing, and behind him he pulls the rest of us; and I want to be there, for every movement, every sound. Why should I want to die away from all that?

[ESTHER *falters.*]

That's made me tired again, that has.

I keep wanting to talk and I keep getting tired.

Lady Othello

Arnold Wesker

Penguin, London 1990

Act 1 Scene 11

ROSIE:

Passion! Men are driven by passions. Makes them irrational. The conduct of political affairs is perverted by irrational men. That'll be my thesis. Surprises you, huh? Coming from a woman who's driven by passions which make her behave irrationally?

[*What follows is calculated to inflame him sexually and impress him intellectually. At the same time.*]

You take protest. Nothing wrong with protest. Sign of a healthy society. What goes wrong? I'll tell you what goes wrong. People! They fuck it up. Start off wanting more democratic rights, end up wanting to overthrow democratic institutions.

You take commerce. People rage against capitalism. Nothing wrong with trading. Healthy instinct. What goes wrong. People! They fuck it up. Get greedy. Produce cheap goods. Form totalitarian monopolies which become a law unto themselves.

You take politics. Nothing wrong with politics. It's the art of government. We have to be governed. Since Adam! So what goes wrong? I'll tell you what goes wrong. People! They become politicians, fuck up politics. Ambitious! Dishonest! Opportunist!

You take religion. Nothing wrong with wanting to believe in a

God. Jesus! Buddha! Muhammad! They're all saying the same thing – be good, love one another, look after the kids! So what goes wrong? I'll tell you what goes wrong. People! They become fanatics. Scream at one another. 'I'm holier than thou and all must be as holy as me!'

You take the study of art. Nothing wrong with that. You can't make the insensitive sensitive but a little bit of analysis here or history there helps! So, what goes wrong? I'll tell you what goes wrong. People! They become critics, professors, journalists – get on ego-trips. Fuck it up! Suddenly everyone's discussing the merits of critics rather than the artist they're supposed to be criticizing. Crazy!

You take science. 'Science will blow up the world! Pollute the earth!' Bullshit! You wanna attack Newton, Galileo, Benjamin Franklin? Science gave me my contact lens and saved Mark dying of diphtheria. So, what goes wrong? I'll tell you what goes wrong. People! Along come the crooked industrialists, the dishonest politicians and the righteous fanatics, and *they* fuck up science.

[*She's finished and beams her full power upon* STANTON *who is sagging.*]

Guess I tired you out, huh? And we haven't even started *tonight's* studies, honey.

The Death of Bessie Smith

Edward Albee

Samuel French, London 1959

Scene 2

NURSE:

I don't suppose you'll drive me to work. I don't suppose, with your headache, you feel up to driving me to the hospital. I didn't think you would. And I suppose you're going to need the car too. Yes; I figured you would. What are you going to do Father? Are you going to sit here all afternoon on the porch, with your headache, and watch the car? Are you going to sit here and watch it all afternoon? You going to sit here with a shotgun and make sure the birds don't crap on it . . . or something? You're going to need it. Yeah; no doubt. You going to drive down to the Democratic club, and sit around with that bunch of loafers? You going to play big politician today? Hunh? You going to go down there with that bunch of bums . . . light up one of those expensive cigars, which you have no business smoking, which you can't afford, which I cannot afford, to put it more accurately . . . the same brand His Honor the mayor smokes . . . you going to sit down there and talk big about how you and your mayor are like this . . . you going to pretend you're something more than you really are, which is nothing but . . . a hanger-on . . . a flunky . . . is that what you need the car for Father, and am I going to have to take that hot, stinking bus to the hospital? You make me sick. I said you make me sick Father.

Snowangel

John Carlino

Dramatist Play Service, New York 1964

CONNIE:

He came to me while I was workin' in a house in Stockton. His name was Paco. He'd come up from the mountains in the south of Mexico ta dig potatoes. I turned a coupla tricks with him. Short times. He was always so quiet . . . and . . . I don't know, kinda gentle. Then he came in one day and paid for the price of a day's work. He took me out into the country. We sat down on a hillside, in the sunshine. He had a bottle of dago red. He started ta talk ta me. It was all fast and crazy at first. Then I understood. It was about his home. There were lakes where men fished with nets in the shape of great, huge butterflies. There were old temples and big snakes and everybody played the guitar and sang and had a helluva good time. And he laughed when he tole me. And the sun hit his teeth. He had a smile that made ya feel like butter. *Damn*, he had a smile! We drank the wine and he went on about the fruits and the colors of things and how great it was ta live with animals, and about all the beautiful churches with gold and silver crosses and saints that came from Spain in the olden days. And the mountains are so high, the snow never melts. Then he said, "Connie, I take you to my home. Caramba, when they see you they will fall down dead. Beautiful. They have never seen such beautiful. Caramba, *mi vida*, you will be the sun and the music and the fire of my house. You will be my blanket. Then you will do this work no more. And we will forget. Ay, Caramba, Connie, we will forget." An' he'd laugh. *Damn*, he had a smile. We lay in the sun all day. An' you know what? He kissed me gently . . . so gently. An' he touched my hair, "Caramba, Connie, how we will forget." He dug his nails inta dirt for a whole week ta buy that day. I waited, but he never came back. Immigration got him. He'd snuck in. They sent him back. I didn't even know his last name. I never saw him again. Little Paco. Paco the Mex. I never loved anybody again. I got busted after that and went to Frisco. And then, after that . . . that was all. [*A long silence, then she looks up at John.*] That's what I remember, mister. That's what I imagine.

Lady and the Clarinet

Michael Cristofer

Dramatists Play Service, New York 1985

LUBA:

Don't give me that crap. You're all the same. Cut from the same piece of chintz. I didn't hear from him again for seven weeks. Seven weeks. Not a phone call. Nothing. Not even a message from his constipated secretary. She was having a field day. Very polite at first. 'No, I'm sorry, Mr. Evert isn't here today. Can I take a message.' Very careful. Trying to sound like she didn't know who I was. Trying to sound like she didn't know that I was the same person who called an hour ago. The same person who called three times yesterday and twice the day before and God knows how many humiliating times before that. I went down there one day. I went right to his office. Face it, I said to myself, get it over with. I went into the building, up the elevator to the desk. The secretary is sitting there, guarding the door. She doesn't know who I am, we've never met. She says, can I help you and I freeze. I'm afraid to talk, I'm afraid she'll recognize my voice if I open my mouth. And even if she didn't, what do I say? 'Can I help you?' she says again. I don't move. Maybe I'm not here, maybe I can disappear. 'Is anything wrong?' she says. And I want to say, yes, something is wrong, yes. I wouldn't be standing here with my tongue in pieces if something wasn't wrong. I stood there in front of the desk, staring at the secretary – she was getting nervous by now – I pulled myself together. Christ, old Jack is not worth losing my mind over. I leaned forward. I put both my hands down on her desk. The secretary leaned toward me. She was ready to listen. I was ready to speak. I was gaining confidence. I said to myself, you're okay now. Everything's fine. I took a deep breath and threw up all over her desk. Confident, easy, in control, lovely to look at, delightful to hold. I always wanted to be like that. I'm a jackass. I do everything ass-backwards. My mother used to say I had the touch of a blacksmith. But I felt better. After that. I felt a lot better. I really did pull myself together. I got back to work. I started seeing somebody else. A plumber. Yeah. No brains. Lots of money. No problems. No expectations. I was on the road to recovery. Back on the track.

The Shadow Box

Michael Cristofer

New York, 1977

AGNES:

Claire is my sister.

[*With great reluctance*] We were very close. Our whole family. Especially after my father died. We were just children then. Mama worked very hard to keep us together. We had a dairy farm.

It was a beautiful place. Big, old house . . . 1873. And so much land. It seemed even bigger then . . . I was so little. We were very happy.

And then Claire . . . there was a boy . . . well, she left us . . . just like that. She was a lot like Mama. They would fight and yell and throw things at each other . . . they got along so well.

Claire was so beautiful, and I would hide in my room. I got so frightened when they fought, but . . . I don't know . . . sudddenly the fight would be over and Mama would throw open her arms and curse the day she bore children and Claire would laugh and then Mama would laugh and hug her close . . . and then all of us, we would laugh . . . I can still hear us . . .

But she left. And we never heard from her. Almost a year. The longest year I can remember. Mama waited and waited, but she never wrote or came back to visit . . . nothing. And then one morning, finally, we received a letter from a man in Louisiana. There was an accident . . . something. And Claire was dead. They said at first they thought she was going to be all right, but she was hemorrhaging and . . . This is very hard to remember.

You see, it was after Claire died that Mama started to get sick. All of a suddden, she was 'old.' And she isn't, you know. But she just seemed to give up. I couldn't bring her out of it. Claire would have. But I couldn't. We lost the farm, the house, everything. One thing led to another.

The letters . . . uh . . . It was after one of the last operations. Mama came home from the hospital and she seemed very happy. She was much stronger than ever. She laughed and joked and made fun of me, just like she used to . . . and then she told me she had written a letter while she was in the hospital . . . to Claire . . . and she said she was very nice to her and she forgave her for not writing and keeping in touch and she asked her to come home to visit and to bring her children . . . Claire had been dead for a long time then.

I didn't know what to do. I tried to tell her . . . I tried . . . but she wouldn't listen . . . And, of course, no letter came. No reply. And Mama asked every day for the mail. Every day I had to tell her no, there wasn't any. Every day. I kept hoping she would forget, but she didn't. And when there wasn't any letter for a long time, she started to get worse. She wouldn't talk and when she did she accused me of hiding the letters and sometimes . . . I didn't know what to do . . . So . . . [*Pause*]
I've been writing these letters for almost two years . . . You're not angry with me, are you?

It means so much to her. It's important to her. It's something to hope for. You have to have something. People *need* something to keep them going.

Sometimes I think, if we can wait long enough, something

will happen. Oh, not that Mama will get better, but something . . .

So I write the letters. I don't mind. It's not difficult. I read little things in books and newspapers and I make up what's happening. Sometimes I just write whatever comes into my head. You see, Mama doesn't really listen to them anymore. She used to. It used to be the only time I could talk to her. But now it doesn't matter what they say. It's just so she knows that Claire is coming.

Death and the Maiden

Ariel Dorfman Nick Hern Books, London 1992

Act 2

PAULINA:

I propose that we reach an agreement. You want this man freed and I want – would you like to know what I want?

. . .

When I heard his voice last night, the first thought that rushed through my head, what I've been thinking all these years, when you would catch me with a look that you said was – abstract, fleeting, right? – you know what I was thinking of? Doing to them, systematically, minute by minute, instrument by instrument, what they did to me. Specifically to him, to the doctor. . . . Because the others were so vulgar, so – but he would play Schubert, he would talk about science, he even quoted Nietzsche to me once.

I was horrified at myself. That I should have such hatred in me, that I should want to do something like that to a defenceless human being, no matter how vile – but it was the only way to fall asleep at night, the only way of going out with you to cocktail parties in spite of the fact that I couldn't help asking myself if one of those present wasn't – perhaps not the exact same man, but one of those present might be . . . and so as not to go completely off my rocker and be able to deliver that Tavelli smile you say I'm going to have to continue to deliver – well, I would imagine pushing their head into a bucket of slime, or electricity, or when we would be making love and I could feel the possibility of an orgasm building, the very idea of currents going though my body would remind me and then – and then I had to simulate it, simulate it so you wouldn't know what I was thinking, so you wouldn't feel that it was your failure – oh Gerardo.

So when I heard his voice, I thought the only thing I want is to have him raped, have someone fuck him, so that he should know just once what it is to . . . And I can't – I thought that it was a sentence that you would have to carry out.

But then I told myself it could be difficult, after all you do need to have a certain degree of enthusiasm to –

So I asked myself if we couldn't use a broom handle. Yes, Gerardo, you know, a broom. But I began to realise that wasn't what I really wanted. And you know what conclusion I came to, the only thing I really want?

[*Brief pause.*]

I want him to confess. I want him to sit in front of that cassette-recorder and tell me what he did – not just to me, everything, to everybody – and then have him write it out in his own handwriting and sign it and I would keep a a copy forever – with all the information, the names and data, all the details. That's what I want.

Beyond Therapy ★

Christopher Durang

Samuel French, New York 1983

Act 1

PRUDENCE:

Do I want to be married? I have no idea. It's so confusing. I know when I was a little girl, Million Dollar Movie showed this film called "Every Girl Should Be Married" every night for seven days. It was this dumb comedy about this infantile girl played by Betsy Drake who wants to be married to this pediatrician played by Cary Grant who she sees in a drug store. She sees him for two minutes, and she wants to move in and have babies with him. And he finds her totally obnoxious, but then at the end of the movie suddenly says, "You're right, you're adorable," and then they get married. [*Looks baffled by the stupidity of it all*]

And what confused me further was that the actress Betsy Drake did in fact marry Cary Grant in real life. Of course, it didn't last, and he married several other people, and then later Dyan Cannon said he was insane and took LSD and so maybe one wouldn't want to be married to him at all. But if it's no good being married to Cary Grant, who is it good being married to?

Act 1 Scene 3

CHARLOTTE:

[*Into intercom*] You may send the next patient in, Marcia. [*Enter* BRUCE. *He sits*]

Hello.

[*Pause.*]

[*Points to child's drawing*] Did I show you this drawing? It was drawn by an emotionally disturbed three year old. His parents beat him every morning after breakfast. Orange juice, Toast, Special K.

Do you see the point I'm making?

Well, the point is that when a porpoise first comes to me, it is often immediately clear . . . Did I say porpoise? What word do I want? Porpoise. Pompous. Pom Pom. Paparazzi. Polyester. Pollywog. Olley olley oxen free. Patient. I'm sorry, I mean patient. Now what was I saying?

Oh I hate this, when I forget what I'm saying. Oh, damn. Oh, damn damn damn. Well, we'll just have to forge on. You say something for a while, and I'll keep trying to remember what I was saying . . .

Ad?

[*Remembering, happy*] Oh, yes. Personal ad. I told you that was how the first Mr. Wallace and I met. Oh yes. I love personal ads. They're so basic. Did it work out for you?

Oh, dear. Oh, I'm sorry. One has to be so brave to be emotionally open and vulnerable. Oh, you poor thing. I'm going to give you a hug. [*She hugs him and kisses him with her Snoopy doll*]

Life is so difficult. I know when I met the second Mr. Wallace . . . you know, it's so strange, all my husbands have had the same surname of Wallace, this has been a theme in my own analysis . . . Well, when I met the second Mr. Wallace, I got a filing cabinet caught in my throat . . . I don't mean a filing cabinet. What do I mean? Filing cabinet, frying pan, frog's eggs, faculty wives, frankincense, fornication, follies bergère, falling falling fork, fishs fork, fish bone. I got a fish bone caught in my throat.

Then we got married, and we had quite a wonderful relationship for a while, but then he started to see this fish wife and we broke up. I don't mean fish wife, I mean waitress. Is that a word, waitress?

No, she didn't work in a restaurant, she worked in a department store. Sales . . . lady. That's what she was.

He was buying a gift for me, and then he ran off with the saleslady. He never even gave me the gift, he just left me a note. And then I was so very alone for a while.

I'm afraid I'm taking up too much of your session. I'll knock a few dollars off the bill. You talk for a while, I'm getting tired anyway.

Oh, don't be afraid! Never be afraid to risk, *to risk*! I've told you about "Equus", haven't I? That doctor, Doctor Dysart, with whom I greatly identify, saw that it was better to risk madness and to blind horses with a metal spike, then to be safe and conventional and dull. Ecc, ecc, equus! Naaaaaaaay! [*For Snoopy*] Ruff ruff ruff!

I think you should put in another ad.

But this time, we need an ad that will get someone more exceptional, someone who can appreciate your uniqueness.

Now let's see. White male, 30 to 35, 6'2" no – 6'5", green eyes, Pulitzer Prize-winning author, into Kierkegaard, Mahler, Joan Didion and sex, seeks similar-minded attractive female for unique encounters. Sense of humor a must. Write box whatever whatever. There, that should catch you someone excellent. Why don't you take this out to the office, and my dirigible will type it up for you. I don't mean dirigible, I mean Saskatchewan.

I know, I mean secretary. Sometimes I think I should get my blood sugar checked.

See you next week.

[*He exits*]

[*Into intercom*] Marcia, dear, send in the next porpoise please. Wait, I don't mean porpoise, I mean . . . pony, pekinese, parka, penis, no not that. I'm sorry, Marcia, I'll buzz back when I think of it.

Laughing Wild

Christopher Durang

Grove Press, New York 1988

Act 1

WOMAN:

Oh, it's all such a mess. Look at this mess. My hair is a mess. My clothes are a mess.

I want to talk to you about life. It's just too difficult to be alive, isn't it, and to try to function? There are all these people to deal with.

. . .

I swung the cab door open and I shouted into his open window, 'Your mother sucks cocks in hell!' Although I think my tongue slipped and I actually said, 'Your mother sucks socks in hell,' which was kind of funny, but I was too angry to laugh; and he just said, 'You're fuckin' nuts,' and he drove off in this terrible hurry, and the tire almost went over my foot, but luckily I fell backwards into the gutter. [*Looks at the audience for a moment.*] Are you following this so far?

So, there I was lying on my back in the gutter, and this street musician came over to me and he asked me if I needed help, and I said, 'No, but can you play 'Melancholy Baby'?' And I thought that that was a pretty funny thing for me to say under the circumstancess, and that I had a fair wit and intelligence even if I had been in mental institutions, and I thought to myself, maybe if this man laughs at my comment, which is wry and peculiar and yet oddly appropriate to the circumstance, that maybe I will have found a companion for the rest of my life . . . this street musician didn't laugh at my comment about 'Melancholy Baby,' he looked at me very seriously and asked me if I was all right, and I said, 'You don't really want to know, do you? You don't want to know how I am really, to hold me in the night, to comfort me in sickness and in health,' sickness caused by the dying of the ozone layer, health caused by . . . well, who knows what causes health, probably sugar is killing all of us, and besides, I hadn't really even gotten a good look at him in the dark, maybe I wouldn't like his looks, he might not be the right person for me to spend the rest of my life with anyway. And then he asked me if I wanted help to stand up or if I wanted to stay seated in the gutter, and I thought to myself, I don't know the answer to that question. And so I said, with a laugh, 'I don't know the answer to that question, ask me another one,' which I thought was kind of a funny remark in the circumstances, this crazy lady in the gutter after she's attacked someone at the tuna fish counter and been assaulted by a taxi driver, sort of gallant and witty in the midst of unspeakable woe.

What is that line from Beckett? 'Laughing wild amid severest woe.'

So then I said to him, with another wry smile, 'I am laughing wild amid severest woe.' And he looked alarmed and then he said, if you need help getting to the ladies' shelter, I'll be over there playing my guitar. And then I knew I'd been fortune's fool, that this man was not meant to share my life with me, he was humorless, he didn't have a sense of shared existential ennui, angst, whatever, I've been to college. Although I didn't read everything they assigned me, of course. What good would it have done? [*Looks at the audience.*]

Do you follow me so far?

Little Murders

Jules Feiffer

New York 1968

PATSY: . . . It's not enough! It's not, not, not enough! I'm not going to have a surviving marriage, I'm going to have a flourishing marriage! I'm a *woman*! Or, by Jesus, it's about time I became one. I want a *family*! Oh, Christ, Alfred, this is my wedding day. [*Pause. Regains composure*] I want – I want to be married to a big, strong, protective, vital, virile, self-assured man. Who I can protect and take care of. Alfred, honey, you're the first man I've ever gone to bed with where I didn't feel he was a lot more likely to get pregnant than I was. [*Desperate*] You owe me something! I've invested everything I believe in you. You've *got* to let me mold you. *Please* let me mold you. [*Regains control*] You've got me begging. You've got me whining, begging and crying. I've never behaved like this in my life. Will you look at this? [*Holds out finger*] That's a tear. I never cried in my life.

You never cried because you were too terrified of everything to let yourself *feel*! You'd have to learn crying from a manual! Chop onions! I never cried because I was too tough – but I felt *everything*. Every slight, every pressure, every vague competition – but I *fought*. And I *won*! There hasn't been a battle since I was five that I haven't won! And the people I fought were happy that I won! Happy! After a while. Alfred, do you have any idea how many people in this town *worship* me? [*To herself, quickly*] Maybe that's the attraction – you don't worship me. Maybe I'd quit loving you if you *did* worship me. Maybe I'd lose all respect for you if you did all the things I want you to do. [*Thinks about it*] Alfred, you've got to change! [*Regains calm*] Listen . . . I'm not saying I'm better or stronger than you are. It's just that we – you and I – have different temperaments. [*Explodes*] *And my temperament is stronger than yours!* [*No reaction*] You're a wall! [*Circles around him*] You don't fight! You hardly even listen! Dear God, will somebody please explain to me why I think you're so beautiful?

House of Blue Leaves ★

John Guare

Samuel French, New York 1971

BUNNY:

I'm not that kind of girl. I'll sleep with you anytime you want. Anywhere. In two months I've known you, did I refuse you once? Not once! You want me to climb in the bag with you now? Unzip it - go on - unzip it - Give your fingers a smack and I'm flat on my back. I'll sew those words into a sampler for you in our new home in California. We'll hang it right by the front door. Because, Artie, I'm a rotten lay and I know it and you know it and everybody knows it -

I'm not good in bed. It's no insult. I took that sex test in the *Reader's Digest* two weeks ago and I scored twelve. Twelve, Artie! I ran out of that dentist office with tears gushing out of my face. But I can face up to the truth about myself. So if I cooked for you now and said I won't sleep with you till we're married, you'd look forward to sleeping with me so much that by the time we did get to that motel near Hollywood, I'd be such a disappointment, you'd never forgive me. My cooking is the only thing I got to lure you on with and hold you with. Artie, we got to keep some magic for the honeymoon. It's my first honeymoon and I want it to be so good, I'm aiming for two million calories. I want to cook for you so bad I walk by the A&P, I get all hot jabs of chilli powder inside my thighs . . . but I can't till we get those tickets to California safe in my purse, till Billy knows we're coming, till I got that ring right on my cooking finger . . . Don't tempt me . . . I love you . . .

Marco Polo Sings a Solo

John Guare

Dramatist Play Service, New York 1977

DIANE:

I really started cookin' when I was eight. I sat down at the piano as I had every day since I could walk, threw back the lid of the Knabe-Bechstein-Steinway and there on the keys was Mozart. I was never lonely playing the piano. Brahms was always there. Bach. Chopin. And here was Mozart. Hi, Mozart! Only this time he had a raincoat on. A little raincoat. Now I had been told to beware of men in raincoats, but after all, it was Mozart. Mozart's no degenerate. Mozart's no creep. You can trust Mozart. The cool water of Mozart. He says, 'Hello, little girl. You gonna bring me back to La Vie?' I said, 'Golly, I'll try.' And I began playing that Kochel listing I had been practising for a year with that magical imitative brilliance that children can have. The technical mastery and total non-comprehension that children can have. I lifted my hands, dug them into the eighty-eights and Mozart says: 'Yeah. Give it to me.' I looked down. Mozart. The raincoat. Opened. The keys became erect. Black. White. I became terrified. Mozart! This isn't a school yard. This is a hall named after Mr. Andrew Carnegie and I'm only eight years old and what the hell are you doing??? 'More. More. More,' says Mozart and he throws back his head. 'Dig those digits into these eighty-eights. Bring me back to life. Bring me back to life.' Mother??? Dad?? They're in the wings blowing kisses at me. Holding up signs. 'You've never played better.' Mozart moans. It's a short piece. It ends. Mozart spurts all over me. I'm wet. Mozart wet. Frightened. The audience roars. This child prodigy. Can't they see what's happened? I look down and hear a chorus of 'yeahs' coming from all those little dead men in raincoats. There's a scuffle and Brahms leaps on the keys. 'Me next! Me next! Bring me back to life.' My fingers dig into Brahms. Well, I started to like it. Mozart lives. Brahms lives. For the next twenty years that was my life. Diane de la Nova and her circus of Music.

Diane de la Nova and her Massage Parlor of Melody.

. . .

It's so easy to get brilliant reviews. You simply sit at the piano every day for twenty years with the moss growing up your legs, sparrows nesting in your hair, bringing dead men in raincoats back to life.

Crimes of the Heart

Beth Henley Dramatist Play Service, New York 1982

BABE:

. . . I realize that he's a black boy, Meg. Why do you think I'm so worried about his getting public exposure? I don't want to ruin his reputation!

I was just lonely! I was so lonely. And he was good. Oh, he was so, so good. I'd never had it that good. We'd always go out into the garage and –

All right, then. Let's see . . . Willie Jay was over. And it was after we'd –

And we were just standing around on the back porch playing with Dog. Well, suddenly, Zackery comes from around the side of the house. And he startled me 'cause he's supposed to be away at the office, and there he is coming from 'round the side of the house. Anyway, he says to Willie Jay, 'Hey, boy, what are you doing back here?' And I said, 'He's not doing anything. You just go on home, Willie Jay! You just run right on home.' Well, before he can move, Zackery comes up and knocks him once right across the face and then shoves him down the porch steps, causing him to skin up his elbow real bad on that hard concrete. Then he says, 'Don't you ever come around here again, or I'll have them cut out your gizzard!' Well, Willie Jay starts crying, these tears come streaming down his face, then he gets up real quick and runs away with Dog following off after him. After that, I don't remember much too clearly; let's see . . . I went on into the living room, and I went right up to the davenport and opened the drawer where we keep the burglar gun . . . I took it out. Then I – I brought it up to my ear. That's right. I put it right inside my ear. Why, I was gonna shoot off my own head! That's what I was gonna do. Then I heard the back door slamming and suddenly, for some reason, I thought about mama . . . how she'd hung herself. And here I was about ready to shoot myself. Then I realized – that's right I realized how I didn't want to kill myself! And she – she probably didn't want to kill herself. She wanted to kill him, and I wanted to kill him, too. I wanted to kill Zackery, not myself 'Cause I – I wanted to live! So I waited for him to come on into the living room. Then I held out the gun, and I pulled the trigger, aiming for his heart, but getting him in the stomach. [*After a pause.*] It's funny that I really did that.

The Wake of Jamey Foster

Beth Henley

New York 1983

MARSHAEL:

All these ties. You never wore even half of 'em. Wasted ties. God, loose change. Always pockets full of loose change. And your Spearmint chewing gum sticks. Damn, and look – your lost car keys. Oh, well, the car's gone now. Damn you, leaving me alone with your mess. Leaving me again with all your goddamn, gruesome mess t'clean up. Damn, you, wait! You wait! You're not leaving me here like this. You're gonna face me! I won't survive! You cheat! I've got t'have something . . . redemption . . . something. [*The coffin is closed. She begins to circle it.*] There you are. Coward. Hiding. Away from me. Hiding. [*Moving in on him.*] Look, I know I hurt you something bad, but why did you have to hold her fat, little hand like that? Huh? Treating me like nothing! I'm not . . . nothing. Hey, I'm talking. I'm talking to you. You'd better look at me. I mean it, you bastard! [*She pulls the lid off the coffin.*] Jamey. God, your face. Jamey, I'm scared. I'm so scared. I'm scared not to be loved. I'm scared for our life not to work out. It didn't, did it? Jamey? Damn you, where are you? Are you down in Mobile, baby? Have you taken a spin t'Mobile? I'm asking you - shit - Crystal Springs? How 'bout Scotland? You wanted to go there . . . your grandfather was from there. You shit! You're not . . . I know you're not . . . I love you! God. Stupid thing to say. I love you!! Okay; okay. You're gone. You're gone. You're not laughing. You're not laughing. You're not . . . nothing. Still I gotta have something. Still something . . . The trees. Still have the trees. The purple, purple trees -

M. Butterfly

David Henry Hwang

New York 1989

RENEE:

You have a nice weenie.

Penis. You have a nice penis.

What - can't take a compliment?

Most girls don't come out and say it, huh?

Most girls don't call it a "weenie," huh?

Most guys are pretty, uh, sensitive about that. Like, you know, I had a boyfriend back home in Denmark. I got mad at him once and called him a little *weeniehead*. He got so mad! He said at least I should call him a great big weeniehead.

There's "cock," but that sounds like a chicken. And "prick" is painful, and "dick" is like you're talking about someone who's not in the room.

I – I think maybe it's because I really don't know what to do with them – that's why I call them "weenies."

I mean, really *do* with them. Like, okay, have you ever looked at one? I mean, really?

It just hangs there. This little . . . flap of flesh. And there's so much fuss that we make about it. Like, I think the reason we fight wars is because we wear clothes. Because no one knows – between the men, I mean – who has the bigger . . . weenie. So, if I'm a guy with a small one, I'm going to build a really big building or take over a really big piece of land or write a really long book so the other men don't know, right? But, see, it never really works, that's the problem. I mean, you conquer the country, or whatever, but you're *still* wearing clothes, so there's no way to prove absolutely whose is bigger or smaller. And that's what we call a civilized society. The whole world run by a bunch of men with pricks the size of pins.

Later

Corrine Jacker

Dramatists Play Services, New York 1979

Act 2

KATE:

I can sail. As well as any man. Better than most. My father taught me – tacking, charting a course, no yawing when I'm at the rudder. Our secret language. Malachai and me at the boat house, while Molly sipped iced tea under her sun umbrella and Laurie's skin shrivelled up in the club pool. A boat needs attention. Scraping, sanding, painting, varnishing. One June day when it was hotter than this, I worked for seven hours straight on the hull, and he hugged me and said no son could've been better. I knew he meant that if a man was going to get stuck with daughters, he might as well have one like me. And he hauled out the thermos with rum and tea in it, and he poured me a cupful, and he said, "Drink it down, you'll feel cold as an icicle." Oh, I did. It turned my veins into refrigerator coils. Goose flesh came out on my shoulders, and down my arms, I started to shiver until my teeth clacked together. But he knew what to do. He rolled the sleeves of my tee shirt down as far as they'd go, and he stuck me into the sun, rubbing my hands together and hugging me to stop me from shaking. And then, he said, "Oh, well, you're a girl after all, aren't you, Katey, honey." And I lay my head against his shoulder and wished there was a way to change that. I never felt that cold again. Not till he was dead, and we were alone, in the viewing room, and the air conditioning was blowing so fiercely. We went out, Laurie and I, to get drunk, having dumped Molly on some cousin or other, and I ordered rum and iced tea, because I wanted to shiver, I wanted the temperature of my blood to go down below zero, so it would freeze and clot, and stop. But I couldn't get away from that music. The beat kept making my heart pump. I got drunk. My God, was I drunk, and my cheeks got red, and the blood kept right on moving. I couldn't get cold enough. I could have taken a bath in ice cubes and I wouldn't have gotten cold enough . . . Well, Katey's a girl after all.

Fear of Flying

Erica Jong

Holt, Rinehart & Winston, New York 1973

ISADORA WING:

Brian Stollerman (my first lover and first husband) was very short, inclined to paunchiness, hairy and dark. He was also a human cannonball and a nonstop talker. He was always in motion, always spewing out words of five syllables. He was a medievalist and before you could say 'Albigensian Crusade' he'd tell you the story of his life – in extravagantly exaggerated detail. Brian gave the impression of never shutting up. This was not quite true, though, because he *did* stop talking when he slept. But when he finally flipped his cookies (as we politely said in my immediate family) or showed symptoms of schizophrenia (as one of his many psychiatrists put it) or woke up to the real meaning of his life (as he put it) or had a nervous breakdown (as his Ph.D. thesis adviser put it) or became-exhausted-as-a-result-of-being-married-to-that-Jewish-princess-from-New-York (as his parents put it) – then he never stopped talking *even* to sleep. He stopped sleeping, in fact, and he used to keep me up all night telling me about the Second Coming of Christ and how this time Jesus just might come back as a Jewish mediavalist living on Riverside Drive.

Of course we were living on Riverside Drive, and Brian was a spellbinding talker. But still, I was so wrapped up in his fantasies, such a willing member of a *folie à deux* that it took a whole week of staying up every night listening to him before it dawned on me that Brian *himself* intended to be the Second Coming. Nor did he take very kindly to my pointing out that this might be a delusion; he very nearly choked me to death for my contribution to the discussion. After I caught my breath (I make it sound simpler than it was for the sake of getting on with the story), he attempted various things like flying through windows and walking on the water in Central Park Lake, and finally he had to be taken forcibly to the psycho ward and subdued with Thorazine, Compazine, Stelazine and whatever else anyone could think of. At which point I collapsed with exhaustion, took a rest cure at my parents' apartment (they had become strangely sane in the face of Brian's flagrant craziness) and cried for about a month. Until one day I woke up with relief in the quite of our deserted apartment on Riverside Drive, and realised that I hadn't been able to hear myself think in four years. I knew then that I'd never go back to living with Brian – whether he stopped thinking he was Jesus Christ or not.

Boy's Life

Howard Korder

Grove Press, New York 1989

LISA:

I'm going to lie down in traffic, Don. I'm going to let a crosstown bus roll over me because my life is meaningless since you betrayed me . . .

"You love me!" That doesn't mean shit! This isn't high school, I'm wearing your *pin*. You want me to tell you what really counts? . . .

It's not worth it! Do what you want, it doesn't matter to me. I don't even know you, Don. After four months I don't know who you are or why you do what you do. You keep getting your dick stuck in things. What is that all about, anyway? Will someone please explain that to me? [*Pause.*] Don't look at me that way.

Like a whipped dog. It's just pathetic.

. . .

[*Pause.*] You don't understand what I'm talking about, do you? You're just afraid of being punished. I'm not your *mother*. I don't spank. [*Pause.*] I'm going. Have fun fucking your bargain shopper and cracking jokes with your creepy friends.

. . .

Wait. Wait. This is not it. This is nothing. I can't even talk to you until you tell me the truth. Why did you do this, Don? When you knew I trusted you? Was it her breasts, her buttocks, the smell of her sweat? Was it her underwear? Was it because she wasn't me? Did you have a reason? Any reason at all?

[*Pause.*]

Would you like to play a little game, Don?

A pretend game. Let's pretend you could do anything you wanted to. And whatever you did, nobody could blame you for it. Not me or anyone else. You would be totally free. You wouldn't have to make promises and you wouldn't have to lie. All you would have to do is know how you feel. Just that.

What would you do?

[*Pause.*]

You'd be . . . different?

Would you?

Different how?

[*He pauses and falls into a long silence.*]

[*Blackout.*]

Angels in America – Part I Millennium Approaches

Tony Kushner

Nick Hern Books, London 1992

Act 1 Scene 3

HARPER:

People who are lonely, people left alone, sit talking nonsense to the air, imagining . . . beautiful systems dying, old fixed orders spiralling apart . . .

When you look at the ozone layer, from outside, from a spaceship, it looks like a pale blue halo, a gentle, shimmering aureole encircling the atmosphere encircling the earth. Thirty miles above our heads, a thin layer of three-atom oxygen molecules, product of photosynthesis, which explains the fussy vegetable preference for visible light, its rejection of darker rays and emanations. Danger from without.

It's a kind of gift, from God, the crowning touch to the creation of the world: guardian angels, hands linked, make a spherical net, a blue-green nesting orb, a shell of safety for life itself. But everywhere, things are collapsing, lies surfacing, systems of defence giving way . . . This is why Joe, this is why I shouldn't be left alone. [*Little pause.*]

I'd like to go travelling . . . Leave you behind to worry. I'll send postcards with strange stamps and tantalising messages on the back. 'Later maybe.' 'Nevermore . . .'

. . .

People are like planets, you need a thick skin. Things get to me.

. . .

I feel . . . that something's going to give. It's fifteen years till the second millennium. Maybe Christ will come again. Maybe seeds will be planted, maybe there'll be harvests then, maybe early figs to eat, maybe new life, maybe fresh blood, maybe companionship and love and protection, safety from what's outside, maybe the door will hold, or maybe . . . maybe the troubles will come, and the end will come, and the sky will collapse and there will be terrible rains and showers of poison light, or maybe my life is really fine, maybe Joe loves me and I'm only crazy thinking otherwise, or maybe not, maybe it's even worse than I know, maybe . . . I want to know, maybe I don't. The suspense . . . it's killing me.

Angels in America – Part II Perestroika

Tony Kushner

Nick Hern Books, London 1994

HANNAH:

I don't have pity. It's just not something I have. I believe people have visions. One hundred and seventy years ago, which is recent, an angel of God appeared to a man on a hill in upstate New York, not far from here and showed him where truth lay buried.

You may not believe that but I do. So listen. This man, who was a prophet, I . . . still believe that, he taught that there is a partnership of action, a marriage of body and spirit struck between Heaven and Earth. He had great need of understanding. His desire made prayer. His prayer made an angel. The angel was real.

You can't imagine. The things in my head. I come from Salt Lake. My son is . . . well, like you. He called me to tell me this. I was mad as blisters, just *furious* and it wasn't really till I had sold the house and I was waiting hours for him in this cold airport and he didn't show that I suddenly had a revelation. That in actual truth I was angry only because he is in his own way so dense and helpless. The way men tend to be. I *should* have been angry about, his . . . sin. [*She shrugs.*] I just couldn't care. Two men together. It isn't a pleasant notion but then, for me, men in *any* configuration . . . well they're so lumpish and stupid.

And stupidity gets me cross.

My point is, it was terrifying. My beliefs had died. And I hadn't noticed, I was distracted . . . I had been carrying around these dead beliefs. They were killing me. And I hadn't noticed that, either.

An angel is just a theory, is what I believe. A belief with wings and arms, that's capable of carrying you. It isn't flesh as we know it, but it is . . .

Embodied, anyway. And so our beliefs are susceptible, as flesh is. To corruption, the loss of glory, and . . . [*She stops.*]

Death.

Blue Window ★

Craig Lucas

Theatre Communications Group, New York 1989

LIBBY:

I went to get my teeth cleaned, of all things. I had thirteen cavities. I wound up . . . seeing lot of . . .

The dentist. Martin Vanderhoffer.

And he was just a lot of fun. His family had a lot of money. I mean a lot, a lot of money, so he didn't have to work at all if he didn't want to, but he liked to which I liked. And he was fun.

And so we started to go out. And I got more involved with Marty. We talked about getting married . . .

Aaaaand we did. Get married.

Big wedding. And . . . we laughed. Marty . . . We bought a big apartment on East 71st Street – much too big for just the two of us. Brand-new building, we had a terrace and windows on three sides. It was almost the penthouse. We'd been married about three months – not quite –. And . . . I think I was pregnant. I was. We talked about it and I was late. Anyway. I could have been . . . And we were standing by the window. I didn't have any clothes on. I was looking out. It was late – late afternoon. Everything was blue – as blue as it can be before it gets black.

And Marty said, Come out on the terrace. I said, I don't have any clothes on. And he brought me this little robe. And we walked out on the terrace.

We'd only lived there two months. And he kissed me and I put my head back to look up at the sky. Our reflections were in the glass. And I put my head back; we lived on the seventh floor, there was another one above us.

And we leaned - he leaned - I set my back against the rail and it . . . just . . . We were gone; we were over. I saw us leave the window. I looked - past him, my hands reached past him to try to hold something, there wasn't anything . . . just blue . . . And I didn't black out. I thought - very clearly . . . This is bad. This is real. And it's true, you see everything pass before your eyes. Everything. Slowly, like a dream, and Marty was . . . Marty was climbing up me and screaming and we turned . . . over . . . once . . . and . . . we went through an awning . . . Sloan's . . . Which saved my life . . . And I broke every bone in my face. I have a completely new face. My teeth were all shattered; these are all caps.

I was in traction for ten months. And Tom came to see me every week. Every day sometimes. Marty's family. Who sued the building I mean, they never even attached it to the wall. It wasn't even attached. It was just a rail - a loose rail. There was another one on another floor, the same thing could have happened . . . I landed on him. I killed him. I can't . . .

It's seven years. I'm thirty-three years old. I can't have anybody hold me. I can never be held.

An Othello

Charles Marowitz

Open Space Plays
Penguin, New York 1974

DESDEMONA:

Wouldn't you have, if you'd had the chance? Not just big, and not just black, but holy and black, strong and black, elegant and black. From a world so warm and sweet, so bred to pleasures and to craft that its smallest pot is a priceless relic, and its simplest peasant, a prince in miniature. A culture we can never hope to understand – except by loving those representatives of it who walk through our trashy white streets like ambassadors from an enchanted land.

Oh, I knew what I was giving up. That was clear as day. A doting, doltish father with one eye on the election-returns and the other on a 'good match'. Locked away like a pearl inside the oyster – in darkness and in agony, working up a sparkle that would catch the eye of some mighty visiting dignitary. All the time hearing *his* tread outside the house; his voice, marshalling troops and giving orders. Standing in the doorway, oafish and dumb like a frightened schoolboy and not a general at all. Eyes saying, dare I speak, dare I touch her hand or brush a strand of her hair. And I, pining to be taken up by those pinion-fingers; pummelled into submission; into something finer, sweeter and deeper than I could have ever been without that fierce caress. Riding his cock like a bronco into a wilderness of thorns that never stung, never smarted, but always yielded to whatever path we cut.

Wouldn't you have, if you'd had the chance? If his arms had lifted you, like a baby into a waiting cradle, and his mouth had eaten away the hunger of a thousand parched summers; days filled with dry flirtations and rough-and-loveless goodnight-kisses. Wouldn't you have? If one night, the dream had sprinted out from under your sheets and stood rock-solid by the foot of the bed saying: Let's! And the hell with everything else! Wouldn't you have?

Talking with . . . 'Scraps'

Jane Martin

Samuel French, New York 1982

WOMAN:

I live in Oz. I see it all. I've even gotten so I can smell it. 'Two or three hours walk along this trail brought Ojo and Scraps to a clear level country where there were a few farms and some scattered octagonal houses, all bright Quadling red and smelling of peppermint.' I can live in that sentence for a full 3 hours. You know what? I like that a lot better than life.

Someday I'll be at the front door when Jack comes home. The Chevette will pull up and he'll have the week's charts, the Southeastern sales figures, the demographics under his arm. And there I'll be to give him a nice kiss, holding the spatula, me, Scraps. 'You certainly are a wonder, my dear, and I fancy you'd make a splendid pin cushion. If you belonged to me, I'd wear smoked glasses when I looked at you.' But I do belong to you Jack. I'm your helpmeet, your homemaker.

The thing that frightens me is I'm getting flashbacks, just like combat or acid.

We had some people over. Jack had bought an Atari. You know, those television computer space games? Asteroids, Space invaders, Cosmic Cadet. God, I hate the sound of it. They were talking about municipal bonds or something. We were all around the T.V. with the pretzel mix. Jenny, Allen, Marty, Turk, Jack, me. And I went to Oz. I was in trouble and I was being rescued from a whirlpool by this Ork . . . a bird with four wings, four legs and a propeller tail, and I guess Jack was talking to me and I didn't answer. He had to shake me. I really didn't know where I was. I ruined his best score in the Atari. I suppose he'll leave me when he finds out. Take the Irish setter. He's the provider. Jesus, I'll have to make a living, won't I? Maybe Ozma will see me in her Magic Picture. Then they'll send the Scarecrow to come and get me and we'll ride the Sawhorse all the way back to the Emerald City. We'll lunch with the Hungry

Tiger and the Cowardly Lion. And the Scarecrow will say, 'Why here's a right curious creation, midway between a ragbag and a rainbow. Why my dear, you are quite bedazzling!' The Scarecrow has the very best brains the Wizard ever made. Perhaps we'll be married.

Hurly Burly

David Rabe

Grove Press, New York 1985

Act 2 Scene 1

BONNIE: He slowed it down. But he didn't slow it down enough. I mean, he didn't stop the fucking car. He slowed it down. Whata you mean, 'he slowed it down?' As if that was enough to make a person feel, you know, appropriately handled. He threw me out of my own slowly moving car and nearly killed me.

I just missed cracking open my head on a boulder that was beside the road . . .

What I wanna know about maybe is you, and why you would put a friend of yours like me in that kind of jeopardy. Why you would let me go with this creep, if I was begging, let alone instigate it, that's what I'm wondering when I get right down to it, though I hadn't even thought about it. But maybe it's having a goddamn friendship with you is the source of jeopardy for a person.

I mean this guy, Eddie, is not just, you know, semi-weird; he is working on genuine berserk. Haven't you noticed some clue to this?

He drove; I listened to the music on the tape deck like he wanted, and I tol' him the sky was pretty, just trying, you know, to put some sort of fucking humanity into the night, some sort of spirit so we might, you know, appear to one another as having had at one time or another a thought in our heads and were not just these totally fuck-oriented, you know, things with clothes on.

What I'm getting at is I did nothing, and in addition, I am normally a person who allots a certain degree of my energy to being on the alert for creeps, Eddie. I am not so dumb as to be ignorant of the vast hordes of creeps running loose in California as if every creep with half his screws loose has slid here like the continent is tilted. But because this guy was on your recommendation, I am caught unawares and nearly maimed. I mean, this guy is driving, so I tell him we can go to my house. He says he's hungry, so I say, 'Great, how about a Jack-In-The-Box?' He asks me if that's code for something. So I tell him, 'No, it's California-talk, we have a million of'em, is he new in town?' His answer is, do I have a water bed? 'No,' I tell him, but we could go to a sex motel, they got water beds. They got porn on the in-house video. Be great! So then I detect he's lookin' at me, so I smile, and he says, 'Whata you smilin' about?' I say, 'Whata you mean?' He says, like he's talkin' to the steering wheel, 'Whata you thinkin'?' or some shit. I mean, but it's like to the steering wheel; he's all bent out of shape.

I smiled, Eddie, it's a friendly thing in most instances, but for him it promotes all this paranoid shit he claims he can read in it my secret opinions of him, which he is now saying. The worst things anybody could think about anybody, but I ain't saying nothing. He's sayin' it. Then he screams he knew this venture was a one-man operation and the next thing I know he's trying to push me out of the car. He's trying to drive it, and slow it down, and push me out all at once, so we're swervin' all over the road. So that's what happened. You get it now?

Eddie, it's a rough century all the way around – you say so yourself, Eddie. Who does anybody know who is doing okay? So this is some sort of justification for us all to start pushing each other out of cars? – things aren't working out personally the way we planned?

. . .

I'm gonna level with you, Eddie, I came here for a ride home and an apology.

Savage Love

Sam Shepard

Faber & Faber, New York 1981

Watching the Sleeping Lover

I wake up
Only a little ways
Out of sleep

You look like my child
Breathe
Helpless sleeper
Frightened of your dreams
Separation of sleep
I breathe with you
Breathe the same way
See how it is to be you
Sleeping
I feel like a detective
Spying
Your sleeping body

I'm not very far from sleep
Your dream changes
Your lips move

Talking to it
In words I've never heard

Then comes a longing
That I don't understand
Because it feels like it's towards you
But here you are
So I don't understand
What this longing's for

I embrace you in sleep
My arm moves with your breathing
Your breath makes my arm rise and fall

For one moment I think of the killing
Still
Frozen

I'm confused by the yearning
I want to have your dreams inside me
I want to strangle your dreams
Inside me

As the light comes through
And the night is turning into day
I want to know I'll die before you
I want to know I'll die before
We aren't lovers anymore

Beggar

Could you give me a small part of yourself
I'm only asking for the tiniest part
Just enough to get me from here to there

Could you give me something
Anything at all
I'll accept whatever it is

Could you just put your hand on my head
Could you brush against my arm
Could you just come near enough
So I could feel as though you might be able to hold me

Could you touch me with your voice
Blow your breath in my direction

Is it all right if I look straight into your face

Could I just walk behind you for a little while
Would you let me follow you at a distance

If I had anything of value I'd gladly give it to you
If there's anything of me you want just take it

But don't think I'm this way with everybody
I almost never come to this
In fact usually it's the other way around

There's lots of people
Who would love to even have a conversation with me
Who even ask me if they can walk behind me

So don't get any ideas that I'm completely alone
Because I'm not

In fact you're the one who looks like you could use a little
company
Where do you get off thinking you have anything to give me
anyway

I have everything I need
And what I don't have I know where to get it
Any time I want

In the middle of the night
In the midddle of the afternoon
Five o'clock in the morning

In fact I'm wasting my time right now
Just talking to you
[*Hums A capella, melody line only no words*]
"I'm in the mood for love."

Opening

Sometimes I would want to reach
My arm would start
Something in my arm would start

Sometimes I would almost reach
Something near my neck would move
And then come back

I wanted something on my face to show
Some sign
Unlock my face
Instead I lock my arms

The head would nod
While you spoke
I wasn't sure about the head
Wasn't sure what it was saying
While I listened
Wasn't sure what you saw it saying
Agreeing or denying

I wanted my mouth to move
To carry something across
Some sign
One eye was going with it

Is this the face that shows me

It was a moment I wanted to be strong
Through the chest
It fell
You saw it falling
I went on as though you didn't
I brought it back

I was wanting to be clear through the hands
While the voice kept talking
I held my face together
My mouth on my hand
Then it dropped
My hands held each other

All the time you saw me

My whole body began to shudder
Everything began to shudder
Nothing would hold still

You tried to show me you didn't see me shaking

You took my hand away from me
And everything stopped

From your fingers I returned
You
You
You
You
[*repeats*]

First Moment

The first moment
I saw you in the Post Office
You saw me
And I didn't know.

The first moment
I saw you
I knew I could love you
If you could love me

You had sort of a flavor
The way you looked
And you looked at me
And I didn't know if you saw me
And there wasn't any question to ask

I was standing with some papers
I started shuffling the papers
But I didn't know what order to put them in

But I figured I wanted to do it in such a way
That it looked like I had some purpose

But I really just wanted to look at your eyes all the time

And you said
Look at me with your eyes
Look at me with your eyes

In that first moment
Your face burned into my dream
And right away I had this feeling
Maybe you're lost
Until now

Maybe I'm lost
Until now

And I thought
Maybe I'm just making this up

But your eyes
Looked like they were saying
Look at me more

I would shuffle the papers
Look at you
My breathing changed

Then I felt something dissolve
I felt there might be a danger
That anything could happen in the next moment
Maybe you would turn away from me

Or you could say
Let's go together
Forever

The Last of The Red Hot Lovers

Neil Simon

Avon Books, New York 1970

ELAINE:

You hypocrite! You soul-searching, finger-smelling, hypocritical son of a bitch! Who are you to tell anybody how to go through life? What would you have done if I came in here all fluttery and blushing and 'Ooh, Mr Cashman, don't put your hand there, I'm a married woman'? Were you going to tell me how much you respect me, admire me and, at the moment of truth, even love me? You know damn well tomorrow you'd be back behind that counter opening clams and praying to Christ I'd never come back in your restaurant. And you know something? That's the way it should be. Forgive me for the terrible, sinful thing I'm about to say but I happen to like the pure physical act of making love. It warms me, it stimulates me and it makes me feel like a woman – but that's another ugly story. That's what I came up here for and that's what you were expecting. But don't give me, 'When I was nine years old my mother ran off with the butcher and I've been looking for someone to love me ever since.' I don't know your problems and I don't care. Keep your savory swordfish succotash stories to yourself. No one really cares about anything or anyone in this world except himself, and there's only one way to get through with your sanity. If you can't taste it, touch it or smell it, forget it! If you want a copy of that speech, send fifty cents and self-addressed envelope –

It's getting late . . . and I have to feed the lion at six.

. . .

Don't waste your time. We're incompatible. You need Joan Fontaine and I need a box of lozenges.

JEANETTE:

There are only indecent people or idiots in this world because that's all I ever see. And that's how I spend most of my day, thinking about things like that. Is it any wonder I take Digilene?

Do you know what the rate of literacy is in the United States? Eighty-six percent. Do you know how many married people have committed adultery? Eighty-seven percent. This is the only country in the world that has more cheaters than readers.

If I were to tell you stories about people you know, people you respect, you would get sick to your stomach right here on this carpet.

You don't see what's going on around you? The lies, the deceit. The stinking, sordid affairs that are going on in motels, in offices, in little German cars.

Do you know Charlotte Korman, big, red-headed, buxom woman, her husband is the Mercedes-Benz dealer in Wantagh? Mel doesn't like her. He doesn't want me to see her. He doesn't want her to be my friend, doesn't want her to come to our house; he can't stand Charlotte Korman . . .

He's been having an affair with her for eight months! I had to stop seeing her three times a week so *he* could see her four times a week. These are the times we live in, Barney.

You know what my proof is? He told me. Two o'clock in the morning, he leans over, taps me on the shoulder and says, 'I've had an affair with Charlotte Korman.' Who asked him? When he tapped me on the shoulder in the middle of the night I thought he wanted *me*! You know what it is to wake up from a sound sleep with no eyelashes and a dry mouth and hear that your husband is getting it from a woman you're not allowed to see for lunch? And you know why he told me, Barney? He explained it to me. We're living in a new guiltless society. You can do anything you want as long as you're honest about it. Aren't we lucky to be living in such a civilized age? In the old days I would have gone to my grave *ignorant* of the wonderful and beautiful knowledge that my husband was spending his afternoons humping Charlotte Korman! . . . When he told me, I didn't say a word. I went down to the kitchen and made myself a cream cheese and jelly sandwich on date-nut bread. And that was the last time in eight months that I tasted food . . . I estimate, going four times a week, I should be through with Doctor Margolies in another year. And then, when we both think I'm ready, I'm going to get in my car and drive off the Verrazano Bridge. In the meantime, I'm very depressed. Excuse me, Barney. Nothing personal, but I don't think we're going to have our affair.

. . .

Some good time you had, heh, Barney? A barrel of laughs, right?

Don't start again, I only got one Digilene left.

Nuts

Tom Topper

Samuel French, New York 1981

Act 3

CLAUDIA:

When I was a little girl, I used to say to her, I love you to the moon and down again and around the world and back again; and she used to say to me, I love you to the sun and down again and around the stars and back again. Do you remember, Mama? And I used to think, wow, I love Mama, and Mama loves me, and what can go wrong? [*Pause.*] What went wrong, Mama? I love you and you love me, and what went wrong? You see, I know she loves me, and I know I love her, and – so what? So what? She's over there, and I'm over here, and she hates me because of things I've done to her, and I hate her because of the things she's done to me. You stand up there asking, do you love your daughter, and they say 'yes,' and you think you've asked something real, and they think they've said something real. You think that because you toss the word love around like a frisbee we're all going to get warm and runny. No. Something happens with some people: they love you so much they stop noticing you're there because they're so busy loving you. They love you so much their love is a gun, and they keep firing it straight into your head. They love you so much you go right into a hospital. Yes, I know she loves me. Mama, I know you love me. And I know the one thing you learn when you grow up is that love is not enough. It's too much and not enough.

Act 3

CLAUDIA:

Wait a second, wait one goddamn second. What is this?

You set me up and then you bring him back to hammer in the last nail? The hell with that.

. . . take him off and put me on the goddam stand, don't whip me with your goddamm rules. While you're playing with your rules, the meter is running out on my goddamn life. Can't you get that I understand you want to help, and I don't want your help? I know the price of your help. I know I'm supposed to be a good little girl for my mother and father, and an obedient and faithful wife to my husband, and stick out my tongue for the doctor, and lower my head for the judge, I know all that, I know what you expect me to do. Look, I am not just a picture in your heads. I am not just a daughter, or a wife, or a hooker, or a patient, or a defendant. Can't you get that? You don't understand the things I do, but I do have my reasons. They're not your reasons, so they're not real to you, but they're real to me. And that's enough. You think giving blow jobs for a hundred dollars is nuts? I know women who suck for a dinner and crawl through shit for a fur coat. I know women who peddle their daughters to hang on to their husbands, so don't judge my blow jobs, they're sane. I knew what I was doing every goddam minute. And I am responsible for it. I lift my skirt, I am responsible; I go down on my knees, I am responsible. If I play the part you want me to play, if I play sick, I won't be responsible.

Poor, dumb, sick Claudia, she's not responsible, the poor, sick thing, she needs our help. I won't play that part. I won't give you that out. I won't be another picture in your heads, Claudia the nut; I won't be nuts for you. Do you get what I'm telling you? Goddam you, do you get what I'm telling you? One more time: He can sign a piece of paper saying I'm nuts, but it's only a piece of paper and I'm not something on a piece of paper. You can't make me go nuts that way, no matter how many times you say it, you can't make me nuts. [*To* JUDGE.] Or you. Get it straight: I won't be nuts for you. [*A silence.*]

Les Belles-soeurs

Michel Tremblay

Translated by John Van Burek and Bill Glassco

Talon Books, Vancouver, Canada 1992

ROSE:

That's right. Life is life and no goddamn Frenchman ever made a movie about that! Sure, any old actress can make you feel sorry for her in a movie. Easy as pie! And when she's finished work, she can go home to her big fat mansion and climb into her big fat bed that's twice the size of my bedroom, for Chrissake! But the rest of us, when we get up in the morning . . . When I wake up in the morning, he's lying there staring at me . . . Waiting. Every morning, I open my eyes and there he is, waiting! Every night, I get into bed and there he is, waiting! He's always there, always after me, always hanging over me like a vulture. Goddamn sex! It's never that way in the movies, is it? Oh no, in the movies it's always fun! Besides, who cares about a woman who's gotta spend her life with a pig just 'cause she said 'yes' to him once? Well, I'm telling you, no fucking movie was ever this sad. Because a movie don't last a lifetime! [*silence*] Why did I ever do it? Why? I should have said no. I should have yelled it at the top of my lungs and been an old maid instead. At least I'd have had some peace. I was so ignorant in those days. Christ, I didn't know what I was in for. All I could think of was 'the Holy State of Matrimony!' You gotta be stupid to bring up your kids like that, knowing nothing. You gotta be so stupid! I tell you one thing. My Carmen won't get caught like that. Because I've been telling her for years what men are really worth. She won't be able to say I didn't warn her! [*on the verge of tears*] She won't end up like me, forty-four years old, with a two year old kid and another one on the way, with a stupid slob of a husband who can't understand a thing, who demands his 'rights' at least twice a day, three hundred and sixty-five days of the year. When you get to forty and realize you've got nothing behind you and nothing ahead of you, it makes you want to dump the whole thing and start all over. . . . But a woman can't do that . . . A woman gets grabbed by the throat and they stay that way right to the end!

Summer and Smoke

Tennessee Williams

New Directions Publishing Group, New York 1971

Scene 11

ALMA:

Yes, I see! Now that you no longer want it be be otherwise you're willing to believe that a spiritual bond can exist between us two!

But I don't want to be talked to like some incurably sick patient you have to comfort. [*A harsh and strong note comes into her voice.*] Oh, I suppose I am sick, one of those weak and divided people who slip like shadows among you solid strong ones. But sometimes, out of necessity, we shadowy people take on a strength of our own. I have that now. You needn't try to deceive me.

You needn't try to comfort me. I haven't come here on any but equal terms. You said, let's talk truthfully. Well, let's do! Unsparingly, truthfully, even shamelessly, then! It's no longer a secret that I love you. It never was. I loved you as long ago as the time I asked you to read the stone angel's name with your fingers. Yes, I remember the long afternoons of our childhood, when I had to stay indoors to practice my music – and heard your playmates calling you, 'Johnny, Johnny!' How it went through me, just to hear your name called! And how I – rushed to the window to watch you jump the porch railing! I stood at a distance, halfway down the block, only to keep in sight of your torn red sweater, racing about the vacant lot you played in. Yes, it had begun that early, this affliction of love, and has never let go of me since, but kept on growing. I've lived next door to you all the days of my life, a weak and divided person who stood in adoring awe of your singleness, of your strength. And that is my story! Now I wish *you* would tell *me* – why didn't it happen between us? Why did I fail? Why did you come almost close enough – and no closer?

You talk as if my body had ceased to exist for you, John, in spite of the fact that you've just counted my pulse. Yes, that's it! You tried to avoid it, but you've told me plainly. The tables have turned, yes, the tables have turned with a vengeance! You've come around to my old way of thinking and I to yours like two people exchanging a call on each other at the same time, and each one finding the other one gone out, the door locked against him and no one to answer the bell! [*She laughs.*] I came here to tell you that being a gentleman, doesn't seem so important to me any more, but you're telling me I've got to remain a lady. [*She laughs rather violently.*] The tables have turned with a vengeance! – the air in here smells of ether – It's making me dizzy . . .

Open a window. – Thank you, that's better. Do you remember those little white tablets you gave me? I've used them all up and I'd like to have some more.